Outtakes has to do with two very important things in your life. One, any problem that you may have and, two, God's Word. **Outtakes** is here to show you how to take any of your problems to God's Word and take out an answer.

God wants you to be at peace with yourself, your Creator, your family, and your world. **Outtakes** meets you where you are (sometimes hurting and sometimes happy) and shows you how to seek God's advice in all you do.

BY **Bill Sanders:**

Tough Turf
*(Almost) Everything Teens Want Parents to Know**
   **But Are Afraid to Tell Them*
Outtakes: Devotions for Guys
Outtakes: Devotions for Girls

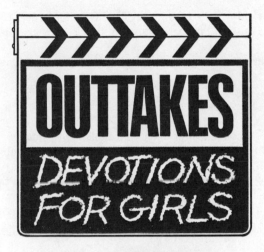

OUTTAKES
DEVOTIONS FOR GIRLS

BILL SANDERS

Power Books

Fleming H. Revell
Old Tappan, New Jersey

Unless otherwise identified, Scripture quotations are from the Holy Bible, New International Version, copyright © 1973, 1978, 1984 International Bible Society. Used by permission of Zondervan Bible Publishers.
Scripture quotations identified KJV are from the King James Version of the Bible.
Verses marked TLB are taken from *The Living Bible*, copyright © 1971 by Tyndale House Publishers, Wheaton, Ill. Used by permission.

Library of Congress Cataloging-in-Publication Data

Sanders, Bill, date
  Outtakes: devotions for girls/Bill Sanders.
    p.   cm.
  Summary: A collection of daily devotions for teenage girls, dealing with such issues as drugs, peer pressure, suicide, and family life.
  ISBN 0-8007-5284-8
  1. Girls—Prayer-books and devotions—English. [1. Prayer books and devotions. 2. Christian life.] I. Title.
BV4860.S26 1988
242'.633—dc19   88-18283
                                                             CIP
                                                             AC

Copyright © 1988 by Bill Sanders
Published by the Fleming H. Revell Company
Old Tappan, New Jersey 07675
Printed in the United States of America

To five great girls in my life:

My sister Nancy, for being God's instrument to share your new found friend and Savior, Jesus Christ, with all of us, over twelve years ago.

My sister Mary, who has been my special angel from heaven, when I couldn't laugh and didn't want to live.

My sister Jean, for showing me what unending faith and belief is all about. . . . We won't quit praying!

My mom, for once again showing us all that God is our source of strength. There is no problem too great for God.

My wife, Holly, who is my best friend. Thanks for loving me when I'm up or down, strong or weak, happy or sad. We'll make it!

Contents

Special Thanks

A special thanks goes to the students of the following schools for filling out hundreds of questionnaires. You gave us the needed information to identify the top problems you and your peers face. Thanks for your willingness and honesty.

Sandusky High School and Sandusky Middle School—Sandusky, Michigan
Westminster Academy—Fort Lauderdale, Florida
House of Hope—Orlando, Florida
Troy City Schools—Troy, Ohio
Mississinewa Community Schools—Gas City, Indiana
Holy Spirit School—Grand Rapids, Michigan
Holy Trinity School—Comstock Park, Michigan
Perrysburg Junior High School—Perrysburg, Ohio
Woodland Elementary—Perrysburg, Ohio
South Middle School and North Middle School—Joplin, Missouri
Croswell-Lexington Middle School—Croswell, Michigan
Pendleton Schools—Falmouth, Kentucky
Hool Elementary School and Heywood Elementary School—Troy, Ohio
Thanks also to the many kids who have written and shared their hurts and feelings with us.

Outtakes would never have been completed without my secretary, Kathy Reisner, and good friend Arla VanDusen's hard work reading through hundreds of students' letters, summarizing them, and compiling them for me. My mom read these letters as well and put them into categories so I could identify the greatest problems. Thanks, Mom. Sandy Bogema edited and put the finishing touches on many of the devotionals, with her thought-provoking one-liners and spiritual stimulators.

But this work would never have been completed had it not been for Kathy Reisner's spending literally hundreds of hours typing and retyping. She was also my constant encourager to stay on target. It's great having someone in my office who loves kids the way Kathy does.

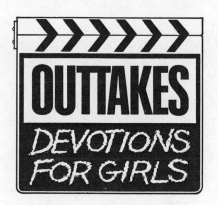

1
A Special Letter

What if you were to come home after school and notice this letter on your bed?

Dear Friend:

As you got up this morning, I watched you and hoped you would talk to Me—even if it was just a few words, asking My opinion or thanking Me for something good that happened in your life yesterday—but I noticed you were too busy trying to find just the right outfit to wear to school. I waited again. When you ran around the house, getting ready for school, I knew there would be a few minutes for you to stop and say hello to Me, but you were too busy. At one point you even had to wait for fifteen minutes, with nothing to do except sit in a chair. Then I saw you spring to your feet. I thought you wanted to talk to Me, but you ran to the phone and called a friend to ask about something that was happening later that day.

I watched you as you went to school, and I waited patiently all day long. With all your activities, I guess you were too busy to say anything to Me. I noticed that before lunch you looked around. Maybe you felt embarrassed to talk to Me, and that is why you didn't bow your head. You glanced three or four tables over in the cafeteria, and you noticed some of your friends talking to Me briefly before they ate, but you didn't. That's okay. There is still more time left, and I have hope that you will talk to Me even yet.

You went home, and it seems as if you had a lot of things to do. After a few of them were done, you turned on the TV. I don't know if I like TV or not. Just about anything goes there, and you spend a lot of time each day in front of it—not thinking about anything, but just enjoying the show. I wait patiently as you watch your TV and eat your meal, but again you don't talk to Me. People seem to come and go but so few have time for Me. As you did your homework I waited. Again, you did what you had to do.

At bedtime tonight I guess you felt too tired. After you said good night to your family, you flopped into bed and fell asleep in no time. That's okay, because you may not realize that I am your special Friend. I've got patience—more than you will ever know. I even want to teach you how to be patient with others as well. Because I love you so much, a long time ago I left a wonderful place called heaven and came to earth. I gave up heaven to be ridiculed and made fun of, and I even died so you wouldn't have to take My place. I love you so much that I will wait every day for a nod, a prayer, a thought, or a thankful part of your heart. I love you so, and I just want you to know that I want to be your special Friend. It is hard when it is only a one-sided conversation and friendship. Well, you are getting up again, and I will wait again patiently, with nothing but love for you, hoping that today you will give Me some time. Have a nice day!

Your friend,
Jesus

If you are like me, Jesus could write that letter to you many days out of the year. Don't let Him write it today or tomorrow. Think about Him. Put Him in your plans, thoughts, and studies. *How would Jesus handle this? Thank You, Lord, for helping me through this.* Look up and say, "You did it again. You sure are my special Friend." Ask Him to help with your memory skills (homework or Scripture); ask Him to give you the strength to call and make up with a friend, congratulate someone you don't know, or meet a new person. You can do it. Your special Friend is waiting to help. He's already told you that in Matthew 28:20 (KJV), ". . . Lo, I am with you alway. . . ." Even if your name isn't *Lo,* Jesus is with you always!

2
The Walk Was the Gift!

Charles Stanley shares the story of a small native boy who brought something to his missionary teacher. As he presented this special gift that showed his great thanks, she realized the little boy had to walk many miles, to the other end of the island, in order to find the shell. "But you had to walk so very far in order to get this," she exclaimed. "That must have taken a great deal of time. I can't thank you enough." The little boy replied, "But you don't understand. The walk was part of the gift."

Look at the price you pay in your walk as a believer. When it comes to being a Christian, maybe you've heard people say, "Our walk is more important than our talk." They mean that if you preach one thing but don't practice it, it becomes meaningless—hypocrisy. Like words without actions, it's no good, shallow, because anyone can do that. The little boy recognized that walking to where he could find this special, rare shell was part of saying "thank you" to his teacher.

When you do things around the house without being asked, or say, "I love you," and, "Thank you," to your parents—you walk your talk. It's the same when you do something for your brother or sister, your teacher, or help out with your best friend's chores.

Share this story with your parents. Then tell them the greatest gift they can give you is to show you firsthand what it is like to walk upright, blamelessly, and with integrity.

Your walk is your gift, not only to the people around you, but to the world. You have no idea how many younger people in your neighborhood look up to you. They watch your every move, see how you react to negatives, problems, pain, and sorrows. They see if you can enjoy life or if you mope around. Give them the gifts of laughter, love, and sharing. Your very walk, your life-style, the way you act, the way you respond, the way you care and share, and the way you pull for your friends may be the most cherished gifts you hand them.

Today ask someone in your life how you can better live up to the standards you love so much. Also share with her how her walk and life-style has encouraged you. Remember, the next time you give a gift to someone that the way you give it, how you prepare for it—not the price tag but the price you paid in love, effort, thought, and concern—really make it a priceless gift, just like the shell from the other side of the island.

Galatians 5:25, 26: Since we live by the Spirit, let us keep in step with the Spirit. Let us not become conceited, provoking and envying each other.

James 1:2, 3, 22: Consider it pure joy, my brothers, whenever you face trials of many kinds, because you know that the testing of your faith develops perseverance. . . . Do not merely listen to the word, and so deceive yourselves. Do what it says.

3
Dream With Me, Please!

Dear Dad: It really hurts me when I tell you things that are really important to me—my feelings and my dreams—and you laugh and tell me they are stupid. I need you to listen and try to understand me. It hurts deep inside when you don't. Your daughter.

Have you tried to share something very important with someone, only to find him preoccupied and uninterested? It is hard to share your desires, dreams, and goals with someone—especially when he doesn't even seem to care. Perhaps his response makes you never want to go to him again. When he asks, "What is that you said?" you feel hurt and say, "It's okay," and you go away and never come back.

If you could write this girl's letter to your dad, would you have the courage? Realize that you have a responsibility to meet your parents, help them understand you, and help them listen. Your relationship with Mom and Dad is too important to let your pride or angry and hurt feelings get in the way—especially if you have other friends whose parents listen to them, take their advice, and are better friends to their daughters than yours are to you. God has given you a practice ground that will train you to deal with people for the rest of your life; you have a great opportunity. While you still have loved ones, a roof over your head, and most of your expenses paid for, please talk things over with your parents. Gently let them know what they don't know. If they don't hear what else you need, they will think they are doing a good job.

Once I heard someone say, "All parents do the very best they can." In most situations I believe that is true. Have your parents ever gotten training in listening and tuning into your problems? Probably not! Have you ever been properly trained in how to present your problems to them, so they will want to listen and help you with a solution? Probably not! In many cases parents get angry because they do not like the way their teens present problems.

When my family and I visited a place for "runaway" and "throwaway" girls, called The House of Hope, several girls told me they left home because their parents couldn't listen, and they didn't know how to keep from being angry with them. Things got worse, fights occurred, and the rest is history. They live in a shelter with other runaways, because they do not know the skills that will help make things right. Finally they've begun to learn them at this place.

When you come to your parents with a problem, share with them that you need them to just be there, to listen, to not give advice until you are completely done, to hurt with you, to keep telling you that they love you and will always be there with you, and that no problem, with God's help, cannot be handled. If you present these points in a loving way—maybe in a letter, if you find that more convenient— your parents will try their very best to follow them. When you feel that no one listens, please take great comfort in realizing that God knows your every thought and listens intently to your every need.

Give your parents the gift of God's lesson:

Ephesians 6:4 (TLB):   And now a word to you parents. Don't keep on scolding and nagging your children, making them angry and resentful. Rather, bring them up with the loving discipline the Lord himself approves, with suggestions and godly advice.

Colossians 3:21 (TLB):   Fathers, don't scold your children so much that they become discouraged and quit trying.

Today go back to Ephesians 6 and read verses 1–3. Before your parents can hear this advice you need to honor and love your father and mother.

4

Green Eyes

Dear Bill: My boyfriend is jealous of me, and he gets so angry if I even look at another guy. What should I do? I feel like I'm in prison. He gets so upset that I worry about what he might do someday.

My dear friend has a very serious problem. If a boyfriend is that jealous of her, it shows serious insecurities, and she needs to ask why he is her boyfriend. However, if she has strong feelings for him and would like to approach him with a suggestion and possible solution and see what choice he makes, I can offer some help.

A story in the Bible tells about jealousy and anger and gives some very wise counsel. However, this jealous guy didn't take the counsel and ended up letting his anger result in murder. Of course it is the story of Cain and Abel.

Both brothers brought offerings to God, but God did not accept Cain's. Cain became very jealous of Abel's offering. Cain got angry, even though he had been at fault in bringing the wrong kind of offering. The amazing thing is this: God came to Cain as this girl can come to her boyfriend. In *Genesis 4:6, 7* (TLB) He warned: ". . . Your face . . . can be bright with joy if you will do what you should! But if you refuse to obey, watch out. Sin is waiting to attack you, longing to destroy you. But you can conquer it!"

Cain had a choice, and so does that boyfriend. His girlfriend has a choice too. No relationship can last if the reins are pulled so tight because of jealousy. If she cannot look at other people while she's young and talk to other people so she can learn how to communicate with people of the opposite sex without getting her boyfriend so mad, angry and jealous, it is a bad situation.

Think of God's suggestion to Cain and ask yourself: *How do I react when someone suggests I have goofed up? Do I deny I have a problem, or do I try to find a solution for it?* God gave Cain a chance to correct his mistake, but Cain refused. Cain's story shows us what can happen to a life and how it can be ruined forever by wrong choices and continued sin. If someone, especially a parent or teacher, points out that you have done something wrong and you need to change it, I challenge you and beg you to take God's way instead of Cain's way. Don't be a wandering fool, like Cain. He ended up a nomad the rest of his life.

Cain's story is told in Genesis 4:1–17. You can also read

about him in the New Testament, Hebrews 11:4; 1 John 3:12; and Jude 11. But for now, concentrate on the gentle and encouraging word God gives Cain to help set him straight. He may be speaking to you in a special area of your life now as well. Go back and read Genesis 4:7 again!

5
Ability Versus Availability

Dear Bill: After hearing you give a talk at our school, I have a question to ask you. I am so very average. How in the world can I ever do a great thing and reach my potential, as you said in your talk? Is it really possible for people of average intelligence, coordination, and so on, like myself, to really do great things, or was it just part of your talk?

Dear Ms. Average: I am so glad you brought this question to my attention, because it is on the hearts of almost everyone. We each look around and see people who seem much more talented, more beautiful, and who have more things going for them than we seem to have going for us. Most of us don't even ask the questions you have: *Can I do great things? Can I really be something special in this world? Can I really make a difference?*

I'd like to show you a couple of examples in God's Word that highlight the difference between what you can do with your own ability and what availability to God will make happen.

In Exodus 3 we read about Moses and the burning bush. God told Moses this was holy ground. He said, "I am the God of your father, the God of Abraham, the God of Isaac and the God of Jacob . . ." (v. 6). In Exodus 3:10 He continues: "So now, go. I am sending you to Pharaoh to bring my people the Israelites out of Egypt."

Like many of us, when we feel something great is at hand, but do not feel capable of doing it, Moses asked, "Who am I . . . ?" (V. 11). Notice how God replied: Exodus 3:12, "I will be with you. . . ." All He wanted was for Moses to make himself available. Moses didn't think he had many abilities. In Exodus 4:10, 11, Moses said to the Lord, "O Lord, I have never been eloquent, neither in the past nor since you have spoken to your servant. I am slow of speech and tongue." The Lord said to him, "Who gave man his mouth? Who makes him deaf or dumb? Who gives him sight or makes him blind? Is it not I, the Lord?" God says, "If you are only available, I will be with you." Exodus 4:15 says of Moses and his brother Aaron: ". . . I will help both of you speak and will teach you what to do."

If you only become available to Him with a heart tuned in to doing good, right, touching lives, and living by integrity and honesty, God will lead the way. He will open the doors and even move your tongue and heart. He will give you a tender conscience. You will know right from wrong and what to do and how to do it. No longer will you wonder how to carry your light, but you have to put God in the center of your heart and your life before you can hear Him calling and leading you.

6
Wisdom From a Teenager

Recently Dr. Norman Vincent Peale spoke in Australia. Before each day's talk they had a prayer breakfast. For two days in a row a young teenager came and shared wisdom far beyond her years. The first day she prayed she shared, "Lord, help me be the person my dog thinks I am." Isn't that a wonderful thought! You know how a dog or any other pet that you have around the house treats you. He thinks you are the greatest! Of course, without you the animal might starve and die, but beyond that he is always loyal and always there. A dog wags his tail; he just wants you to be nice. He thinks you are the most fantastic person in the world. If you have a pet cat, she comes up and rubs against your leg, purrs, and just wants to be petted. Animals want us to take care of them and to be there, much like a little child. "Help me be the person my dog thinks I am"—I think that is wonderful.

The next day she said something that was even more beautiful, in my book. She said, "Lord, help me grow flowers so I don't have to depend on anyone else's bouquet." Do you see the wisdom behind this? She wants to learn how to be happy on her own—how to find life's secrets and answers, so she doesn't have to depend on outside circumstances or other people.

When I was growing up I often asked my mom, "What does this word mean?" She did me the greatest favor of all when she said, "Look it up. Find out for yourself and learn in the process. Grow and learn to read while you learn what this word is. Find out two or three more facts while you are digging it up." In so many words, my mother was telling me to grow my own flowers and not to just let her tell me the meaning of the word or to explain the beauty, definition, or wisdom of a certain phrase or word.

There are really two kinds of people, when it comes to flowers and bouquets. One kind has a great day if everything goes smoothly, if the people around him are happy, if the weather is fine and sunny, if it's Friday, if he just got a good grade on his test, or if his paycheck just came in the mail. Another kind has a good day during the rain. She makes the best of every situation. If she has a problem, she looks for the opportunity in it. If it is cloudy out, she knows that above the clouds there is sunshine.

Do not depend on other people's bouquets, but grow your own flowers—with all kinds of beautiful colors, like the flower of happiness (give it to someone today) or the flower of kindness (find someone who needs kindness desperately and give it away). Don't do it wanting anything in return, but do it just to see the smile on his face and to know deep in your heart that you helped someone less fortunate. Give away the flower of beauty (tell someone how beautiful she is or how nice her new sweater looks). Give away the flower of love (tell someone near you that you love him). Give away the flower of a needed phone call (call a friend and tell her that you need her and want to talk to her).

Flowers come in all sizes. Be the person your dog wants you to be—that your pet thinks you are. Isn't that a great thing for a teenager to say? I think it is a wonderful thing for anyone to say, but especially a teenager. I've got faith in you and your generation, especially if you lean on God. With Him all things are possible. Become wise and ask the Lord to help you be the best person you can possibly be. Maybe it is the person your mother and father think you can be—I know it is the person that your Lord wants you to be. Be wise today and make the world a better place for someone else. You will find that the sun shines brighter on you, too!

Luke 1:37:   For nothing is impossible with God.

7
The Romans Road

Just about every Christian has heard of the Romans road—the pathway of salvation outlined in the book of Romans. Many people have said that if they had the choice of just having one book of the Bible to live with forever, it would be Romans. We will go through this book to discover some exciting truths that can help each one of us feel better about ourselves and our position in Christ. It may help you rediscover what a wonderful gift you have in salvation, lead someone else to Christ, or make a decision for Him, yourself. For the first time you may realize just where you have come from and where you are going.

The Romans road goes from our sin state to being saved in Christ. Romans 1:16 is its start: "I am not ashamed of the gospel, because it is the power of God for the salvation of everyone who believes. . . ." When Paul states that he is not ashamed of the gospel, he means he is proud of it and will stand on it until death, if he has to. One thing, more·than anything else, should be the bottom line for everything we do in our lives: God's Word. God is no better than His Word. He is just and true. He is incapable of lying. If He says it, it must be. Why should we be proud of the gospel? Because it is the power for salvation of everyone who believes.

In my Bible I have 3:10 written in the margin right by Romans 1:16. This way I know the verse that comes next, when I am sharing with someone. "As it is written: 'There is no one righteous, not even one.'" Beside that verse I have 3:23: "For all have sinned and fall short of the glory of God." These two verses merely show that every single person who has ever lived—other than Christ—has sinned. I doubt if you can find any person who can say that he or she has really met someone who has never, ever sinned or made a mistake. Besides putting our faith in the gospel, we must all realize we have fallen short of God's glory on our own. If a person can't recognize that he has made mistakes and has sinned on his own, he will never recognize the need for Christ.

The next verse that I have in the margin is 5:8: "But God demonstrates his own love for us in this: While we were still sinners, Christ died for us." These are amazing and powerful words. While we were still sinners, God sent Jesus Christ to die for us. Not because we were good enough, not because we earned it, but because He loved us that much. Whenever you wonder about God's love for you, remember this: He loved you even before you turned to Him and even when you were turned *from* Him.

From Romans 5:8 I turn to 6:23. This pivotal verse shows us the two ways in which we can go in life. Even though we know that we are sinners, even though we know Christ can save us, even though we know that God loved us so greatly, we still have a decision to make. That decision leads to a destiny. "For the wages of sin is death, but the gift of God is eternal life in Christ Jesus our Lord."

This verse has two parts. The first deals with the wage—a payoff, something we earn by our actions, something we earn and deserve by our way of life. "For the wages of sin is death. . . ." *Death* here means "spiritual death." The payoff for living in our sin and not doing anything about it is eternal separation from Christ. It is called hell. The other part of this verse is beautiful: ". . . but the gift of God is eternal life in Christ Jesus our Lord." Notice the word *gift*. It is the opposite of the word *wage*. A gift is free; you cannot pay for it. You can only be thankful because of it. Someone must buy a gift. Christ paid for our gift of salvation by dying on the cross. We cannot earn it, nor can we be good enough to keep it. Just like a gift at Christmas, God's gift of eternal life or salvation is free—and it's also for anyone who will ask.

Romans 8:28 promises: "And we know that in all things God works for the good of those who love him, who have been called according to his purpose." If we love God, we accept His Son. If we have been called according to His purpose, He touches our hearts, we discover Christ for ourselves, and we ask Him to be our personal Lord and Savior. God's Word says all things that happen to us will work out for good. You see, He will give us the creativity and insight to find the good in everything that happens to us. When negative and terrifying things happen to us, we will realize what God wants us to learn through them. How exciting to know that as a child of God every single thing in your life is planned! All that happens has a purpose, and there is beautiful goodness in it.

To make sure you have this beautiful thing called salvation, to be in the right heart state, to realize that all things that happen to you in the future will work for the good, do what it says in Romans 10:9: ". . . Confess with your mouth,

'Jesus is Lord,' and believe in your heart that God raised him from the dead, [and] you will be saved." God only requires two things: First, He wants you to tell someone that Jesus is the Lord of your life. Second, you have to have faith in that. If you truly believe in your heart that God raised Him from the dead, you *shall* be saved.

I think God did not have video machines back when Jesus was alive because He wanted us to have total faith in things like the virgin birth and the death on the cross. Even seeing Christ's suffering and love in person doesn't prove everything. Thomas, who had been with Jesus for three years, had to see before he could believe in the Resurrection. He had to feel the nail holes; he had to feel Christ's hands and side. We, too, must have faith. If we believe He was raised from the dead and say, "Jesus is my Lord," we shall be saved.

Once we confess Christ and believe in His death and resurrection, we have this beautiful gift called salvation, but the Romans road doesn't stop here. Romans 12:1, 2 tells us how to live as a Christian: "Therefore, I urge you, brothers, in view of God's mercy, to offer your bodies as living sacrifices, holy and pleasing to God—which is your spiritual worship. Do not conform any longer to the pattern of this world, but be transformed by the renewing of your mind. Then you will be able to test and approve what God's will is—his good, pleasing and perfect will."

In those verses God covers all four areas of life: physical, spiritual, social, and mental. God shares how we should grow as physical people: ". . . offer your bodies as living sacrifices, holy and pleasing to God. . . ." Because they only hurt God's temple, we do not choose to put drugs, alcohol, and tobacco into our bodies.

We should also become "holy and pleasing to God. . . ." God wants us to live so that our spiritual beings (the way we conduct ourselves) please the Lord. Notice this means pleasing to *God* and not necessarily to *us*.

"Do not conform any longer to the pattern of this world. . . ." We are social creatures, but God wants us to realize that His salvation makes us different from the world. If we have Christ in our hearts, we are saved. Anyone who rejects Christ is not saved. God does not want people to sit on the fence. Revelation 3:15, 16 warns: "I know your deeds, that you are neither cold nor hot. I wish you were either one or the other! So, because you are lukewarm—neither hot nor cold—I am about to spit you out of my mouth." God says that if we are in the middle, thinking halfway about living like Christians and living in the world the other half, He would just as soon spit us out of His mouth. God wants us to be dedicated.

God covers the mental when He says to renew your mind. God's Word is so important, because it keeps healing, renewing, building, and strengthening us. God's Word is our sunshine, the rain that helps us grow, and the very energy that keeps us alive.

There you have the Romans road. You can turn to these pages any time you need to lead someone to the Lord. Once he has heard these things, he must make a decision. All he needs to do is say a simple prayer, stating in his own words that he realizes that everyone is a sinner, including him. He must recognize that God's Word says if he stays in his sin state, the wage of this sin is death. Show him that he needs to ask God for this beautiful thing called eternal life, recognize that what He did on the cross covers the sin, accept what He did, and ask Him into his heart as his personal Savior. What a wonderful gift you could give someone . . . the gift that is free . . . the gift of eternal life.

Next time, when the road you are traveling seems rocky and things are not going well, turn back to the Romans road and walk through a few of its steps to realize just how fortunate you are!

Just fill in the blank with your name. "I, _____, realize that I have sinned many times and hurt You, God. I am very sorry. I've read Your Word and know that You died for my sins. You paid the price for each and every one of my sins. Please come into my heart and be my Lord and Savior for ever and ever. I love You, Jesus. Amen."

8
Mistakes Can Be Costly

An Associated Press report told about a police officer who got a call from an elderly woman, saying that she needed help, because she was on the floor of her apartment and couldn't get up. She gave the man her address, and the phone went dead. In the confusion at the police station that evening, the officer forgot the call. The next morning the woman was found dead in her apartment. His mistake was very costly, since he could have saved her life.

Did you know that we also make some very costly mistakes? What you do today can scar your memory forever. The things that you will do this weekend at whatever party you go to can leave you in a daze for the rest of your life.

Recently I heard of a man who went home after a party where he had been drinking. He shouldn't have driven, but he did—and went head-on into an entire family. Everyone in the family died, but he is alive. He was okay—except for the memories that will haunt him for the rest of his life.

All the time I talk with young girls who got carried away at parties, got pregnant, had abortions, and have had to pay the cost. Not only did their mistakes cost human lives, they influenced the mothers' self-esteem and respect for the rest of their lives.

Some mistakes are just another way of trying something. If we don't make *some* mistakes, we will never grow, we won't stretch out, and we won't change. The student who is afraid to raise her hand and offer a suggestion or give an answer even though she doesn't know it is right doesn't grow, doesn't challenge herself, and doesn't enlarge her comfort zone. The parent who doesn't read and find out how to have family sharing sessions never improves communication within the four walls of his or her home.

If you want to know what mistakes not to make, look in God's Word. If He says not to do something, then don't do it. You won't have to pay the price. You won't have to live with the memory. You won't have to look back year after year saying, "I wish I had listened." If God says to do something, you can do it. You won't have to worry about bad consequences. God will forgive you if you make a mistake, but some mistakes don't give you a second chance, because you die from them. Even if God forgives you, the pain, the memory, the guilt, and the shame that go along with them may never leave you. But remember that when God forgives us, we are to forgive ourselves as well. We also are to forget it. Completely! God has!

God's Word tells us of one woman who certainly wished she never made her last mistake:

Genesis 19:14–17, 26:   So Lot went out and spoke to his sons-in-law, who were pledged to marry his daughters. He said, "Hurry and get out of this place, because the Lord is about to destroy the city!" But his sons-in-law thought he was joking.

With the coming of dawn, the angels urged Lot, saying "Hurry! Take your wife and your two daughters who are here, or you will be swept away when the city is punished."

When he hesitated, the men grasped his hand and the hands of his wife and of his two daughters and led them safely out of the city, for the Lord was merciful to them. As soon as they had brought them out, one of them said, "Flee for your lives! Don't look back, and don't stop anywhere in the plain! Flee to the mountains or you will be swept away!" . . . But Lot's wife looked back, and she became a pillar of salt.

9

A Fragile Seashell

Naomi Rhode, one of our nation's greatest communica-tors, recently spoke before the National Speakers Association meeting in Charleston, South Carolina. As she talked about professionalism among speakers, she mentioned that earlier that morning, when she put on her precious lapel pin with a gorgeous seashell on it, the shell cracked, breaking into many pieces. Though she felt bad, she also knew there had to be a lesson there somewhere. The shell broke because it was so very fragile, she shared. Then she asked, "How many of you have fragile shells around you that are breakable?" Many of us have what is called a jealousy shell, she told us. We look at other people and we become jealous. Because of this we never feel secure or at peace with ourselves; we always shatter.

Several years ago I stayed away from the National Speakers Association for two years. These are my friends and peers. At these meetings I learn how to become a better speaker and writer; I learn how to market my skills; contact schools; reach young people, parents, and teachers, yet I stayed away for two years. Why? Because of my jealousy shell. I would always look around at others, who seemed to be doing better, having more fun, knowing more people—and I couldn't handle it. It was easier for me to stay home than to confront them, share with them, or be happy for them.

Do you have a thin, glasslike wall surrounding you? It might look okay from the outside, but from the inside you know it is so breakable and you're easily hurt. Get rid of your jealousy shell. Be thankful for what you've got. Look at yourself from the inside out. Develop character qualities that will make you strong and durable.

Part of Naomi's shell—the firm foundation it was glued onto—did not break. Make your foundation firm and solid by putting God first, your family second, and your jealousies, desires, perceptions, and need to be popular third. Then you won't break like that little shell. Be strong today, and be careful how you walk, so you don't break another shell as well.

Instead of having faith in a breakable and expendable shell, today place your trust in a firm, strong, durable stone:

Isaiah 28:16:   So this is what the Sovereign Lord says: "See, I lay a stone in Zion, a tested stone, a precious cornerstone for a sure foundation; the one who trusts will never be dismayed."

1 Corinthians 3:11:   For no one can lay any foundation other than the one already laid, which is Jesus Christ.

Unlike Naomi, you won't have to worry about going in front of people with your jewel shattered. That is, of course, if you put your trust in the cornerstone and not just fancy, shiny jewelry.

10
I Still Need a Dad

Dear Dad: I remember, when I was younger, we always used to play ball together and do other things. Now it seems as if I don't even have a father, because I never see you. You leave for work before I get up for school, and I am in bed by the time you come home. It seems as if you are so busy that you don't have any time for me. These are the toughest years of my life. I need you now more than ever, Daddy. .

In the hundreds of letters girls write their dads, a common thread runs through many: Dad spent much time with them when they were little girls, but now that they have become teens, Dad seems to have disappeared. Every story has two sides, of course. Many things enter into this. As teenager you are changing and want to be independent and alone. You couldn't imagine willfully letting your father or mother kiss you in public, could you? They take this pulling away, when you are around your friends, as a rejection of them personally. It is hard for parents to realize that becoming a teen now isn't the same as it used to be.

I see a desperate need today, for teens (especially girls) to fall back in love with their fathers and for fathers to do the same with them—to have fun again, to be there for each other when they need each other. Dads need their daughters as much as daughters need their dads. That takes one giant four-letter word: *time*. When you spend time with me, I know you love me, but when you don't, I wonder why.

Do you feel as if you don't have a father? Do you wonder why he always keeps his appointments for his business associates and his golf game, but he never seems to write down the times you need to spend with him? If this is the case, I strongly urge you to talk to him. Write a letter, if you must. Let him know how much you love him and need him through these next few years. Let him know you need someone to hang on to—a strong shoulder, a mighty hand like that of God's to look up to and hold on to when you are afraid and lonely.

I am asking you to take the first step. Your parents are trying to make ends meet, keep the family going, and pay the bills. They may not know that you have this need, hurt, and emptiness inside you. Go to your dad and let him know how much you love and need him. Do it today, before it is too late. Then, as God says, you will surround him with a sweet-smelling aroma. Who can ignore that?

Ephesians 4:32:   Be kind and compassionate to one another, forgiving each other, just as in Christ God forgave you.

Ephesians 5:2:   And live a life of love, just as Christ loved us and gave himself up for us as a fragrant offering and sacrifice to God.

11
Different Standards for Guys and Girls?

Seventeen hundred high-school kids in a jammed-packed auditorium listen to my friend John Crudele, "Just Say No" expert, speak. He asks the girls, "What do you call a guy who has had sex several times?" He makes sure that they answer him, and they say something like, "A stud," or, "A hunk."

Then he goes to the guys and says, "What do you call a girl who has had sex several times? Come on . . . I want to know." Most of the guys sit there and don't say anything, but he persists: "Tell me. What do you call a girl who has had sex several times, and the word is out around school that she's been around a little bit?" Finally he gets some brave ones who say, "Do you really want us to tell you?" He says, "Yes, I want to know right now." Then they say, "A sleeze," or, "A slut."

John says, "You've got it. Isn't that the way it goes? Look, girls. Realize what is being done here and what is being said. If a guy has been around a little bit with other girls, he is made out to be a hero and the big shot on campus; but any girl who messes around and has sex before marriage is considered a slut or a whore. These statements should make you sick to your stomach for trying to keep up with peer pressure."

Then John asks the guys, "How many times would you want your future wife to have had sex with other people before you marry her—one, two, three, four, five times? If you become a parent and have a daughter, how many times would you want her to have sex before she gets married— three, five, ten times? How many? How about your mother, guys? How many times would you want her to have had sex before she had sex with your father . . . five, ten, fifteen, twenty? How many?" All of a sudden an entire audience of young people, for the first time in their lives may get hit between the eyes with the fact that God says premarital sex is wrong, and it hurts you if you do it. There is no right way to have sex before marriage. You cannot have "safe sex," because nothing will save you from the low self-esteem, the memories that haunt your mind for the rest of your life, as you compare your wife or husband with all your previous lovers. You are not safe from the facts that condoms do not protect you from many venereal diseases, that AIDS is 100 percent deadly, that Dr. Ruth does not care about your life and is not standing on any moral principles whatsoever, and that just because Planned Parenthood says everyone does it, I say, "So what?" They are talking just as Satan would if he were talking to you. I challenge you to greatness. I challenge you to be worth waiting for.

When will the world wake up? When are you, as a young lady with a life ahead of you, going to realize that what you do today puts a scar on your mind forever? Memories don't go away; quite often they last a lifetime, haunting and belittling us. They give us guilt and pain. You can avoid that by standing on God's principles today. Don't give in just because everyone else does. Don't be everyone else!

Guys, if you think you are a stud or the cool dude around

campus because you have been around a little bit and had sex with women, look at one of the strongest men in the whole Bible—Samson. He was God's hero for a moment, but he lusted after beautiful women who had nothing to do with God. They were unrighteous, but he didn't care. His hormones and his desire to fulfill his feelings caused him and the entire nation to suffer because he tried to satisfy his inner feelings, desires, and motives, instead of thinking about right and wrong—what God desired

Read Judges 16 to find out where Samson's weakness really lay. It wasn't in losing his hair, but in being enticed by a woman because of lust. Delilah tricked Samson three different times, and Samson had become so blind to her tricks that he never suspected that she would do it again. Following our desires does that to us: We get blind, we follow no matter what, we forget about God and all the pain that will lie ahead of us.

Judges 16:4, 16, 17, 19, 21:   Some time later, he fell in love with a woman in the Valley of Sorek whose name was Delilah. . . . With such nagging she prodded him day after day until he was tired to death. So he told her everything. "No razor has ever been used on my head," he said, "because I have been a Nazirite set apart to God since birth. If my head were shaved, my strength would leave me, and I would become as weak as any other man." . . . Having put him to sleep on her lap, she called a man to shave off the seven braids of his hair, and so began to subdue him. And his strength left him. . . . Then the Philistines seized him, gouged out his eyes and took him down to Gaza. Binding him with bronze shackles, they set him to grinding in the prison.

12
Thank You, Lord, for Forgiveness

I sure am thankful that the Lord is full of a beautiful thing called forgiveness. At times, however, each of us feels that we have done something unforgettable—and unforgivable.

I would like to look at *forgiveness* today and tomorrow. Today, we'll focus on the positive assurance that God can forgive us totally—no matter what we have done, no matter what we have thought, no matter what we've been a part of in the past. Tomorrow we will look at how we, as examples of Christ, can forgive others.

We keep going to God's Word when we want to find evidence about what He thinks on a certain subject, because God, like us, is no better than His Word. If God says something, He will do it:

Isaiah 44:24, 26: "This is what the Lord says—your Redeemer, who formed you in the womb: I am the Lord, who has made all things, who alone stretched out the heavens, who spread out the earth by myself, . . . who carries out the words of his servants and fulfills the predictions of his messengers. . . ."

When God says He will do something, He does it. When He says He will forgive us, He means exactly that.

But God goes a step farther than forgiveness. He also totally forgets our sins. In Isaiah 43:25 God promises: "I, even I, am he who blots out your transgressions, for my own sake, and remembers your sins no more." It's not as if God gives us grudging forgiveness; He does it eagerly. He *wants* to blot out our sins and even says that He remembers them no more. Once He forgives, He forgets. That is the difference between God and man. Quite often we easily forgive somebody, but we never seem to forget it. We keep remembering and haunting that person with the memory, over and over again—but *not* God. He blots out our sins. Imagine anything that you feel totally ashamed of doing as a mark on a sheet of paper. God comes down with a giant jar of ink and blots it out, covering it totally. The ink is thick and indelible; you can't see through it or wipe it away. It actually soaks through the paper, and the solid blot area is a dark blue spot. In the same way God completely forgets and blots out our sins. If you don't forget someone's sin against you, you haven't totally forgiven her. Forgiving means forgetting.

Isaiah 55:7 points out that we, too, have to do something: "Let the wicked forsake his way and the evil man his thoughts. Let him turn to the Lord, and he will have mercy on him, and to our God, for He will freely pardon." If we will turn to Him away from our sin, He will give us pardon, as though the sin never happened. All we have to do is to turn to God. He has done everything else. When He died on the cross, He paid for all the sins in the whole world—every past, present, and future sin.

Jeremiah 31:34: ". . . For I will forgive their wickedness and will remember their sins no more."

Hebrews 10:17: Then he [the Holy Spirit] adds: "Their sins and lawless acts I will remember no more."

I have heard it said that the one thing that God cannot do is to remember the sins He has forgiven and forgotten. Have you ever wondered where God puts our sins and past troubles once they are forgiven?

Micah 7:18, 19: Who is a God like you, who pardons sin and forgives the transgression of the remnant of his inheritance? You do not stay angry forever but delight to show mercy. You will again have compassion on us; you will tread our sins underfoot and hurl all our iniquities into the depths of the sea.

He crushes our sins under his foot and throws them into the deepest part of the sea! And He doesn't want us to go fishing for them. They are out of season forever more!

Before he traveled overseas, a man found out where they had charted the deepest part of the ocean. Right at the point where the boat crossed it, he started shouting, "Hallelujah, hallelujah, glory be to God." Amazed, people asked, "What are you doing?" He answered, "I'm thanking God, for this is the spot where He buried my sins."

God throws our sins so far from Him that Psalms 103:12 says, "As far as the east is from the west, so far has he removed our transgressions from us." Please spend a few moments today taking a deep breath, relaxing, and just thinking about the wonders of God and His ability to give us this blessed gift of forgiveness. Once you have accepted Christ as your personal Savior, your sins have been forgiven. They are gone, no longer remembered by God. Today accept this challenge: *Don't remember them either. Look forward and move ahead.* God took your sins away in the first place, to prepare you for eternity and for a life on earth in which you can make this a better place for someone else. His hugs come through our arms—His love through our hearts.

43

13
Our Chance to Give

Yesterday we found out that God forgives and forgets, but why can't we? Maybe we can sometimes, but it seems that when a person really hurts us or cuts us deeply, we hang onto those memories far too long. My twins have taught me this lesson. If we have a fight and I get angry at them, a few minutes later they are playing happily in the other room, forgetting what had just happened. Then they come bounding out of their room, with great big smiles and say, "La lu, Daddy!" That is their way of saying, "I love you, Daddy." They put their arms around me and want to wrestle some more, go play a game, or to have me read a book to them. Sometimes I still feel mad at the fight we had forty minutes before, but my kids keep on teaching me a lesson. I call it the three fs: *forgive, forget* and move *forward*.

One mother told me she and her teenage daughter had just had an argument that ruined the mother's entire evening. A few minutes later the daughter was on the phone, talking with a friend, laughing, and making plans for the weekend. "Why can't I forgive and forget that easily?" asked her mother.

Each one of us has the ability to forgive other people. You and I are made in God's image and likeness, and God is a forgiving God. "Made in God's image" doesn't mean we look exactly like Him, but that we have His characteristics and attributes. We can love, we can care, we can hate, we can be just, we can honor, and we can forgive.

Think of someone who has done you wrong. It was her fault, she may have done it on purpose, and you have every right, if you chose it, to be angry at her. God has every right to be angry at us forever, too, but remember what we found out yesterday in Micah 7:18: ". . . You do not stay angry forever but delight to show mercy."

Though God could stay angry, He doesn't. He delights, He enjoys, He loves it when He has a chance to show His mercy for us. We can do the very same thing. No matter how hard your deep hurt is, if you stay angry, it will choke the very life out of you. Anger, bitterness, and worry actually deprive you of excitement and enthusiasm. I've known people who have stayed angry at family members for years. They've never gone back. The hurt and the pain is far too deep to carry.

The other day I played basketball with some friends, who didn't throw me the ball for the entire game. I felt angry with my best friend for two or three days. What a silly way to go through life! I play basketball because I don't do it well, and I want to engage in activities where I am not the star, so I can learn humility and how to give and take.

Pray that God will give you the strength and the courage to forgive someone today. Send that person a note. It will mean the world to you. Just last week my older brother Joe sent me a note forgiving me for a time when I wronged him, and it meant the world to me. I've put that note in a file I call, "the greatest moments of my life." It gives me courage to go back and see that my brother has forgiven me, which makes it easier for me to forgive others. Give away that beautiful gift today, to someone who is waiting, hoping, and praying you can forgive past wrongs.

Matthew 6:14: "For if you forgive men when they sin against you, your heavenly Father will also forgive you."

14
Heroically Unselfish

Vicky Brown of Bloomington, Indiana, can teach each one of us a lesson about being unselfish. Sixteen years ago her sister needed help. Vicky came to her rescue and gave Fran one of her kidneys. That's right, her unselfishness saved her sister's life.

Any regrets? No—none at all—even after the odds have turned against her. The doctors said that the odds were less than 1 in 10,000 that Vicky would ever need a kidney transplant herself, but now she needs one. Her kidney started to fail this past summer, sixteen years after her sister received the transplant. Vicky says, "I felt very good about giving Fran a chance to live. I could never have lived with myself if I hadn't given her my kidney." Today, three times a week, Vicky Brown spends four hours on a dialysis machine.

Doctors could never have predicted that this would happen to Vicky, but it has. With a beautiful unselfish spirit, she has responded to suffering—no regrets, no anger, no bitterness toward her sister—only thankfulness that she could help at the time. In this day and age of brothers and sisters having fights by the hour, because it is the thing to do, we can take a wonderful lesson from Vicky Brown. She helped her sister and saved her life. Now that her life is in danger, she remains filled with peace about the decision she made before.

Each of us has areas in our lives in which we can help somebody. But what if we help him, and it hurts us a little bit? What if we give her a ride and have to go out of our way, and we end up a few minutes late for a meeting? Are we angry about it, or do we feel up because of the good we've done? What if a brother or sister needs help on a project or homework? Do we help, even if we've got things to do ourselves? Our parents help us many times when they are busy. Do we pass this along?

When I read the USA Today article, it mentioned that Vicky Brown had just left her job, because she was unable to stand, bend, or lift much. She is confined to a bed. We all like to think of ourselves as unselfish and caring individuals, but I wonder how I would feel if I were in that bed and had given up part of myself for someone else, and that was why I was sick and hurting now. I pray that if that ever happens to me, I will have the same attitude as this wonderful hero about whom I have read in the newspaper: Vicky Brown.

Luke 10:27–37:   He answered: "Love the Lord your God with all your heart and with all your soul and with all your strength and with all your mind"; and, "Love your neighbor as yourself."

"You have answered correctly," Jesus replied. "Do this and you will live."

But he wanted to justify himself, so he asked Jesus, "And who is my neighbor?"

In reply Jesus said: "A man was going down from Jerusalem to Jericho, when he fell into the hands of robbers. They stripped him of his clothes, beat him and went away, leaving him half dead. A priest happened to be going down the same road, and when he saw the man, he passed by on the other side. So too, a

Levite, when he came to the place and saw him, passed by on the other side. But a Samaritan, as he traveled, came where the man was; and when he saw him, he took pity on him. He went to him and bandaged his wounds, pouring on oil and wine. Then he put the man on his own donkey, took him to an inn and took care of him. The next day he took out two silver coins and gave them to the innkeeper. 'Look after him,' he said, 'and when I return, I will reimburse you for any extra expense you may have.'

"Which of these three do you think was a neighbor to the man who fell into the hands of robbers?"

The expert in the law replied, "The one who had mercy on him."

Jesus told him, "Go and do likewise."

15
The Most Important Decisions of Your Life

Between the ages of seventeen and twenty-three you will make many of the most important decisions of your life. Most likely you will decide who you will marry, what profession you will enter, what education you will have, if you will become an alcoholic or an abuser of drugs and chemicals, and who your close friends will be. Many of your lifelong habits will become ingrained during these vital years.

During this time, most young people go to college or start a career. They get a job and their own apartments. Often they also fall away from God.

In addition young people may fall away from their parents. Just out of high school, they want to become independent. He wants to be on his own, so he moves away. She feels angry at her parents for telling her what to do; she thinks they've pushed her around and never given her thoughts of her own or freedom or trust, so she goes out and sows her wild oats. Both teens discover the world.

Many young people make major decisions during these years, without their parents' or God's help—only to find themselves married. In their early twenties they have marriage problems, self-esteem problems, work problems, and maybe even a first divorce—not to mention drugs, alcohol, and so on.

Include God and your parents during these most vital and important years, I beg of you. Don't do it alone! Life is too tough alone, especially when you have to make decisions that will affect you the rest of your life. Having sex during these years could result in a pregnancy and an abortion and many memories that will never leave you.

Driving too fast without seat belts, using drugs, and so forth can all cause scars that will never fade. Be smart about it, and don't make these decisions without your parents— and most important, the Lord.

Going it alone merely shows that you are like everyone else. Life is too important and you are too special to try to handle it by yourself. If you act on only seventeen or twenty years of experience, the people whom you contact through-out your lifetime will never be touched in a special way. Use the wisdom of God and the wisdom and experience from your parents. God wants to lead the way for you— especially during these difficult years.

Proverbs 6:22, 23: When you walk, they will guide you; when you sleep, they will watch over you; when you awake, they will speak to you. For these commands are a lamp, this teaching is a light, and the corrections of discipline are the way to life.

Psalms 119:9: How can a young man keep his way pure? By living according to your word.

Joshua 1:8: Do not let this Book of the Law depart from your mouth; meditate on it day and night, so that you may be careful to do everything written in it. Then you will be prosperous and successful.

If you are hurting from a past mistake or need God near for a present decision you must make, call on God as the Psalmist did in Psalms 102:1, 2: "Hear my prayer, O Lord; let my cry for help come to you. Do not hide your face from me when I am in distress. Turn your ear to me· when I call, answer me quickly."

16
The Red Light Is On

Gary Smalley, one of the most exciting and helpful speakers I've ever heard, has a message called "More Than Your Cup Can Hold." It deals with you and me and a thing we often want so dearly—happiness. Gary tells of the many ways we try to "fill our cups." We try people, popularity, being part of the group, and so on. But people let us down. When we need them the most, they often fail us or are just plain too busy. Women get married, and their husbands drill little holes in the bottom of their happiness cups. Few husbands seem to be the expected knights in shining armor—I know, because I was supposed to be one. Then women have kids. They feel children will make them complete and fill their cups. But as Gary points out, kids drill giant holes in their cups.

People won't always make us happy, so we try places, forgetting that wherever we go—there we are! Remember, only those who don't get to travel think it's marvelous. Yes, the grass is always greener but it still has to be mowed!

If it's not places, it must be things. A bigger house, the most expensive outfit, car, or boat. People love things.

People, places, things. None of these make us happy forever or through every situation and feeling. Only God can do that. Each of us has a heart, not one shaped like the present you got for Valentine's Day or like the one you draw in school, with an arrow through it. No! It's in a very different yet specific shape: the shape of Jesus. Only He can completely and significantly fill it. God made people to know God. Go to your local bookstore and ask for one of Gary Smalley's books. He'll touch your life in a special and practical way.

Read about this mystery of God in Ephesians 3:14–20.

Ephesians 3:19: And to know this love that surpasses knowledge—that you may be filled to the measure of all the fullness of God.

Isaiah 41:10: "So do not fear, for I am with you; do not be dismayed, for I am your God. I will strengthen you and help you; I will uphold you with my righteous right hand."

Isaiah 43:2: "When you pass through the waters, I will be with you; and when you pass through the rivers, they will not sweep over you. When you walk through the fire, you will not be burned; the flames will not set you ablaze."

Remember, unlike people, places, or things, God will always be with you and protect you if His Son, Jesus, has a home in your heart.

17

Date Rape

Date rape: Are these just words that rhyme, or are they reality for many young people? One of your classmates may not be going out anymore; she's withdrawn and real quiet. Later you find out she was raped on her third date with a guy.

One of the guys in another class has the girls chasing him all the time. He has an angry temper, but halfway through the semester no one is going out with him, and no one is talking either. Later you find out that he habitually plans to rape a girl on the second or third date.

It happens without consent, and believe it or not, date rape accounts for 60 percent of all rapes. Most take place in the person's home, often not on the first date, but on the second or third. Nor does this happen by accident, because two young people get excited and carried away. An article in the January, 1988, issue of *Group* magazine states that 71 percent of date rape is planned. Quite often this violent crime goes unreported because the rapist makes the victim feel guilty; therefore, only about 5 percent of these cases are reported to the police. Still, each year more than 82,000 date rapes are reported.

If you know a victim of date rape, be her friend and follow this advice. Remember that healing takes an awful lot of time. Victims are scared and quite often feel guilty, so they don't know how to reach out. A great deal of shame is heaped on your friend. Be caring and supportive. Help her find someone to talk to, so she can get her feelings out in the open. Get her the proper help, so she can feel secure and confront the issue and the person who performed this violent act against her. Be her team member as God directs you to. Help her accept God's forgiveness, if she finds it hard to do. Also, be careful what you walk into, so you don't have to end up running.

The Bible has much to say about sexual sin, because God knows our deep desires. If you are dating someone, and you are fairly sure that you are going to get carried away, talk about it. Pray about it. Confront the issue. Write down your goals. Before you get involved emotionally, get too carried away, and cannot say "no," talk about the temptation. Don't compromise.

1 John 1:9: If we confess our sins, he is faithful and just and will forgive us our sins [that means *all* sins, including sexual impurity] and purify us [you will be made clean as though you were a virgin in God's eyes] from all unrighteousness.

Yes, you heard me right. If your virginity was taken from you by force, you are still a virgin in your heavenly Father's eyes. He has forgiven you. He knows it wasn't your fault. Forgive yourself. Talk to God and a professional biblical counselor.

18
Too Much to Live For

Every now and then each of us gets a telephone call we wish we hadn't received—usually because we don't like to hear what the other person has to say. A while back I got one of those calls from a friend, who shared a story of his friend's teenage son, who had just committed suicide.

The boy, who seemed to be a high achiever, went to a highly rated college. He appeared to have everything going for him, yet he took his own life. The day before he committed suicide, he made a simple everyday mistake. My friend explained that they think this boy had nothing to live for because he did not know how to tell his father that he had goofed up! My insides hurt while I listened and tried to help in any way I could, and I could only think that this boy had so much to live for. Even more I hurt at not knowing his spiritual condition.

Who's Who Among American High School Students recently conducted a survey dealing with high achievers and suicide. Of the 1,943 students surveyed, 31 percent of high school juniors and seniors who were high achievers had considered suicide.

The factors contributing most to suicides are:

Feelings of worthlessness	86%
Feelings of isolation and loneliness	81%
Pressure to achieve	72%
Fear of failure	61%
Communication gap with parents	58%
Drug and alcohol use	58%
Actual failure	56%
Lack of attention from parents	50%
Lack of stability in the family	49%
Fear for personal future	41%
Unwanted pregnancy	32%
Divorce	24%
Sexual problems	23%
Financial concerns	14%

Reprinted by permission from GROUP Magazine, copyright 1987, Thom Schultz Publications, Inc. Box 481, Loveland, CO 80539.

Of these fourteen factors, notice the one way up top . . . the feeling that I am worth nothing. Can't you see how most all of the rest of these problems directly relate to a person's self-esteem and feeling of worth?

You don't have to be part of these statistics. You've read the factual breakdown, but you don't have to "break down" as you live your life. Tomorrow we'll consider some of the other factors in more detail.

Romans 5:8:   But God demonstrates his own love for us in this: While we were still sinners, Christ died for us.

Jesus loves you so much that He died for you even when you were a sinner. God's love should give you great worth. Read the first three chapters of my book Tough Turf for step-by-step guides to raising your self-esteem.

19
Beyond Suicide

Here are some other factors that cause suicide: Zero in on your weakness and take it to the Lord, who can make you strong!

Feelings of isolation and loneliness: You won't feel lonely or isolated if you like yourself, because you won't mind being with yourself.

Pressure to achieve: If you feel self-worth and enjoy a healthy self-esteem, you usually won't feel much pressure to achieve. You'll do your best and enjoy the day. You'll live for the moment—not tomorrow—and won't worry about yesterday, either.

Fear of failure: Never worry about failure, because it is just a part of life. Everyone fails at some things. Babe Ruth struck out more times than any other person in baseball at the same time that he held the record for the most home runs.

Communication gap with parents: If you feel good about yourself, you will communicate with your parents, because you will recognize that they have weaknesses in this area, too. You will understand that if you find talking to your parents difficult, it is also probably hard for them to listen to you or to talk back and share their concerns and worries.

Drug and alcohol use: If you like yourself, especially if you have Jesus Christ living in your heart and believe that your body is truly a temple of the Lord, you won't put drugs and alcohol into your system. You would not want something to go into your body that will kill thousands of brain cells every instant.

Actual failure: Don't let it bother you a bit. It is a part of life.

Lack of attention from parents and stability in the family: This won't really bother you. If you want more attention from your parents, you might have to first give them some attention. If your family isn't stable, you can't take responsibility for your parents, but you can help add to the family stability by doing what you can to make it a stronger unit.

Fear for personal future: You'll never worry about this if you feel good about yourself. You might plan for your future. You might dream about what you would like to do, but you don't waste time worrying or being full of fear. It is a wasted exercise.

Unwanted pregnancy: Respect yourself and other people too much to ever engage in premarital sex. Believe in God's rules and His law. Who cares what *Playboy*, *Penthouse*, or *Hustler* says or what the TV portrays? Psalms 24:1, 2 says, "The earth is the Lord's, and everything in it, the world, and all who live in it; for he founded it upon the seas and established it upon the waters." What the people in the movies do as a way of life doesn't matter at all. There is God's way, and every other way is not His way. Being different is okay, because you *are* different with the Lord living in your heart.

If God has blessed you by making you a high achiever, don't let the worries and frustrations of this world cause you to focus on your problems and not what He has given you. The specialness that allows you to achieve above what many of the rest of us can should be used for His glory and benefit.

Take a moment and open your Bible and read Philippians

4:4–9. Notice how Paul, who was in prison, taught how to be full of joy. He gives the key to getting away from worry: pray more. Imagine not having to worry about anything! It seems impossible, because most of us worry at school, when we work, about our relationships with others. In verse 7 Paul shares how to have real peace. It comes from knowing that God is in control and that because we have a relationship with Jesus Christ, our destiny is secure and our victory over sin is certain. Let these words fill your heart and help you focus on the good things. Never again point your thoughts at feelings of worthlessness. The reason is simple: You've got too much to live for.

The solution is simple: Focus on the problem solver (Jesus), not your problems!

20
My Father's Arms

She signed it *Empty*, and she called the poem "My Father's Arms." Because I don't know who she is or how to get in touch with her for permission to use her hurting words, I'll share the thoughts she poured out on paper.

She wrote about how much a girl needs her father's arms to cry on and to hang on to, but her father's arms were used for pain—not protection. Her father's arms caused her to cry, not laugh, hurt instead of heal. In her last two lines, she told how often she had cried, and how she has finally said good-bye to her father's arms.

She must have experienced more than physical abuse, and I cried as I read her words from her broken heart. Girls need their fathers in a very special way; fathers need their daughters sometimes even more. When I ask my little Emily to share my four favorite words, she says softly from the heart, "I love you, Daddy." Then I feel as if I am in heaven.

Do you know your father's arms? Does he know yours? Hug your dad if you are blessed to have one. Tell him how much you need his arms to come to and be held in.

If you, like Empty, need your "Father's arms," read Colossians 3:12–15.

Colossians 3:13: Bear with each other and forgive whatever grievances you may have against one another. Forgive as the Lord forgave you.

21
It's All My Fault

"Why are my parents breaking up? I feel as if it's my fault. I seem so empty inside. Why do I have to cry myself to sleep each night?"

Divorce is all around us; it hurts so many people in so many ways. Getting divorced has become so easy, and many couples have the attitude, "If it doesn't work or if we have trouble, we'll get a divorce."

I don't want you to go through the pain of divorce, but even more important I don't want you to suffer the pain of thinking your parents' breakup is your fault. Many teens of broken marriages think they somehow caused the parents' problems and they should be able to fix it.

Realize that the problems your parents may be having are not your fault. Don't blame yourself. The divorce rate is above 50 percent. That's right—over half of all marriages end in divorce. Kids didn't cause all these. The parents did! Adult people have adult problems.

Every divorce has a unique set of problems, but the number-one cause is a lack of communication: parents not talking, listening, or sharing their hurts, fears, and joys. Finances also cause major stresses on marriage. Many couples spend 110 percent of what they earn. Busy schedules and both parents working can also contribute to the problem. When you spend eight to ten hours outside the home, working as hard as you can, it's hard to come home and make the marriage work when you feel physically and mentally shot.

Spiritual problems are another major cause of divorce. If God's two most important commandments are not followed, how can any relationship stay healthy? (Read Matthew 22:37-39.) When Christians love God (and want to glorify Him in all they do) and love their spouses as themselves, marriages will last. Billy Graham says he never has to worry about divorce—to him, it's not even an option.

Satan's greatest challenge and his greatest successes lately have been in breaking up families. Don't let him break yours, and don't let him put the blame on your shoulders. Pray hard for your parents, that they will stay together. If they don't, pray that they will find Jesus personally through this. Claim Romans 8:28. If you can't get rid of the pain, at least get rid of the blame.

22
Outside Looks Versus Inside Feelings

I am a downhill snow skier. I love the sport, and have recently taken it up again. In Colorado, a couple of years ago, I took some lessons from an expert Swiss skier. The whole time, I kept asking him, "Are my feet close enough together? How do I look? What do you think of my skiing style?" He noticed that I feel most comfortable when I ski with my skis about ten inches apart, and he kept asking me, "How do you feel when you ski like that?"

"I feel great, but how do I look?"

"It's not important how you look. . . . It is how you feel," he responded.

The instructor went over the basics, showing us how to bob up and down as we went around the corners; telling us not to stay crouched, so we wouldn't get cramps in our legs and would have a smooth flow, a feeling of being like a snake weaving back and forth down the hill, with effortless motion. Finally, by the end of the lesson, which was several hours long, I realized what he meant. Why should I waste my time worrying how other people think I look? Instead, I should concentrate on the euphoric feeling I get when I master that hill and do it with confidence and without falling.

What that ski instructor told me that day is also a pretty good lesson in life. We have two ways to go through life: (1) Worrying about what other people think about us, how we look to them. Are our clothes just right? Are we in style? *Do I have the right tan, hair color, or hair-style? What about my car? Am I up on the latest fads and fashions, and do I know the latest jargon? Do I know the scores of the week before and all the teams?* (2) We can go through life feeling good inside, because of what we believe, how close we stay to the people we love, as well as our God—our Creator. We feel good inside when we know that what we do matches what we believe.

The people who feel the best inside have great peace in their hearts, usually because they know who they are, why they are here, and where they are going. They don't have to pretend to be anyone they are not. Because they live in the now, they do not worry about yesterday or concentrate on what they will do tomorrow. Instead they enjoy the moment. If they see flowers nearby, they smell and enjoy them. When they see a child, they stoop down. They don't care if the other kids move on. Like the TV ad that shows a fellow using slow-moving ketchup, and all the other guys in the car say, "Hurry up. We're going."

"I'll be there in a minute," he answers, waiting for the ketchup to slowly drip out of the bottle onto his french fries.

If you've seen the ad, you know what happens. The carload of his buddies drives away, laughing, thinking they've left him behind. After he gets done with his ketchup, a carload of girls comes and picks him up. As they drive by each other downtown he has the last laugh.

When you feel good inside, you don't worry about having to please other people as much as yourself. You also never please yourself by doing something that would hurt another person, help him lose his respect, or help her destroy any part of your body or her body. Feeling good inside means having a presence that says, "I'm glad to live in the here and now. I wouldn't want to live in any other time in history, because in this day and age I have the opportunity to influence more people than any other time that the world has ever known."

The next time you go down the ski slopes of life, looking from side to side and getting a crick in your neck, wondering what other people think of you and how you look on the outside, remember the advice from that great skier whom I met in Colorado: How you feel on the inside will get you down the hill in style, with confidence and composure, not the color of the outfit on the outside. Happy skiing.

Matthew 6:25–27: "Therefore I tell you, do not worry about your life, what you will eat or drink; or about your body, what you will wear. Is not life more important than food, and the body more important than clothes? Look at the birds of the air; they do not sow or reap or store away in barns, and yet your heavenly Father feeds them. Are you not much more valuable than they? Who of you by worrying can add a single hour to his life?"

23
A Lesson From Joey

Some friends in my Sunday-school class have an autistic child. With a group of caring fellow classmates, I signed up to watch eleven-year-old Joey, to free his parents from having to constantly watch him.

Autism is a lifelong disability, primarily characterized by slow development or lack of physical, social, and learning skills. Often a child has an abnormal response to sensations such as sight, hearing, touch, pain, balance, smell, and taste. Autism is different from mental retardation and mental illness. Joey can carry on a conversation with you, just like one of your classmates, except his interest span only lasts a few minutes—or seconds. He can be totally with you, then totally gone.

When I was with Joey yesterday, I learned some very valuable lessons. The first is that of patience. Joey's mom and dad came in about ten minutes late and shared with a chuckle that Joey was in a playful, kidding mood. He was playing games with them and wouldn't get out of the car in the church parking lot. He just laughed and refused to do it. It seemed fun to him at the time, so he just wouldn't leave the car for about ten minutes. As they shared I noticed they weren't angry, bitter, or stress filled. They realized that their son, whom they love very much, isn't perfect and that somehow, somewhere, God has given them the beautiful patience to put up with it and to grow with him. With my own three normal children I find it so easy to get angry and let stress completely control me and my emotions. Whenever I think of Joey's mom and dad, I regain some strength and courage and say, "God, I know that if You can hang the moon in the sky and cause a beautiful flower to grow, You can give me the patience I need to be a hero to my kids."

The second gift that Joey gave me was the gift of laughter. You never really know what he is going to say, so you flow with him wherever he wants to go. He came in and wanted to pretend I owned the grocery store and he owned the hardware, and we exchanged bread for tools. About two minutes later he pretended we were both buying donuts from Dunkin' Donuts. I wanted to make the lesson a little bit spiritual, since that was the reason for my being with him, so I said, "Joey, Joey." This caught him a little off guard. I asked him, "Who was born on Christmas Day?" He said, "Jesus." Then I asked, "Who rose from the dead on Easter day?" He said, "Joey Baker." We both just cracked up. His timing was perfect. He knew the right answer, but he shouted out his own name. We just laughed together, and I hugged him—and usually he can't even be touched. I felt like an eleven-year-old right with him. A few minutes later I noticed a little wood carving of the name *Jesus* on our pastor's desk, in his office, where I was spending this time with Joey. I held it up and said, "You've seen this before, haven't you, Joey?" He said, "Yep!" I said, "What does it say?" He shouted back, "Arby's." We had another great laugh.

I got back home after church, and the Lord had a quiet little talk with me. He said, "If Joey's mom and dad can have that kind of patience, and if Joey can laugh and enjoy life with such beauty and ease in his shape, you can certainly handle your problems, whatever they might be, as they come up."

Let's take Joey's lesson today and be patient with somebody whom we don't understand or who gets on our nerves, and somehow, somewhere, let's cause someone to laugh and enjoy life just a little bit more because we were there. *Thanks, Joey. I love you.*

2 Thessalonians 3:5 (TLB):   May the Lord bring you into an ever deeper understanding of the love of God and of the patience that comes from Christ.

Psalms 126:2: Our mouths were filled with laughter, our tongues with songs of joy. Then it was said among the nations, "The Lord has done great things for them."

Notice in the first verse that the love of God comes before patience, and in the second verse we are to be filled with joy and laughter by remembering the great things God has done for us. Make a list of the great things God has done for you.

24

Answered Prayer

Does the Lord really answer prayer? Quite often we don't believe He does, so we don't pray with much confidence. When you are in need or desperate, prayer comes easily, but to pray as a way of life, even when things are fine, and to know deep in your heart that God hears you and will answer you, is a beautiful thing.

One night I gave an after-dinner talk to some business people. My normal comfort zone is teens, parents, and teachers, so I felt a bit nervous speaking to a bunch of business people. After a long cocktail hour (I mean a *real* long cocktail hour), there was a group of definitely drunk people in the back of this room, which held about one hundred. The drunks were loud and boisterous, and they wanted everyone to know it. I started and talked about eight to ten minutes, but this group still would not get quiet. They would not shut up; they would not have any courtesy at all, and they made life miserable for me. In their laughter and jeers, the talk was getting muffled. Just about the time I got ready to put them down and say something smart like, "Give me my chance to talk now, and you can talk later," or, "Would one of you like to stand up and give us a report about the meeting you are having right now?" or, "Do you desperately need something else to drink? If you do, there is a bar across the street." I leaned on the podium, which was small and made out of tin, sitting on top of the table. As I did that the podium crashed to the tabletop, in about five different pieces. It broke the ice in such a way that the head of the group went over and asked the loud table to be quiet. I fixed the podium, we had a good laugh, we talked about making the best of negative situations like the one I was in, and the rest of the talk went wonderfully. Just a little while later, I realized that the podium breaking was a gift from God. He allowed me to hold my tongue—not to put someone down. He came to my rescue in an amazing way.

I don't believe in coincidences—especially not for God's children. He watches over us, and He knows every hair on our heads. Do you think He wants me to look bad in front of a group, especially when it is my livelihood? Absolutely not! Do you think that He wants you to make a fool out of yourself in front of your friends? No! He wants us each to be a strong stage person for Him—a witness—someone who makes other people say, "I want to be like you. Where do you get your strength from?" God allowed me to do that in an amazing thing called breaking the podium at the right moment. If you don't think God wants you to shine, read about how you are a light, in Matthew 5:14–16.

Look in your past. I think you will see that if you asked, God came to your aid and rescued you right when you least expected it and when you most needed Him. Count on Him today to do the miraculous and amazing. That is what He is there for!

Mark 11:23–25: "I tell you the truth, if anyone says to this mountain, 'Go, throw yourself into the sea,' and does not doubt in his heart but believes that what he says will happen, it will be done for him. Therefore I tell you, whatever you ask for in prayer, believe that you have received it, and it will be yours. And when you stand praying, if you hold anything against anyone, forgive him, so that your Father in heaven may forgive you your sins."

Matthew 21:22: "If you believe, you will receive whatever you ask for in prayer."

Luke 11:9, 10: "So I say to you: Ask and it will be given to you; seek and you will find; knock and the door will be opened to you. For everyone who asks receives; he who seeks finds; and to him who knocks, the door will be opened."

I believe the greatest prayer we can ever pray is "Dear God, let Your will be done in this situation." Sure, we want the pain to stop. If God thinks that is best for us, He *will* allow it to stop. Remember the Twenty-Third Psalm, when you pray. Verse 4 says, "Even though I walk *through* the valley of the shadow of death, I will fear no evil, for you are with me; your rod and your staff, they comfort me" *(italics added)*. The key word is *through*. God will be with us as we go through our problems. He won't keep all troubles and pains from us, but He will never leave us during those hard-to-understand times.

25
Popularity at All Costs

How important is being popular to you? Really think about it. Is it more important for you to look good in your friend's eyes—or the eyes of people you don't even know—than it is to look good in God's eyes? Let's say that you are in school. Everyone competes to get attention, and people want to sit next to the certain popular ones. They want others to notice them at all costs. How important is it to you?

What about your clothes? Your mom says she will not buy designer jeans, no matter what. If you want jeans, you will have regular jeans—the cheap kind. How important are clothes to you?

What about the Friday-night party? You know the host is providing a keg of beer, or you've been asked to bring a six pack. All the kids who you really want to know will be there. What would you do?

What about the dating game? Everyone has a date on Friday night, except you. How do you feel inside? What can you do about it?

Stop for a moment and read Matthew 23:11, 12. This describes God's way of being great. What do you think about it? Do you really believe that serving other people will gain you more friends in the long run—and the right kind of friends—if you do that instead of always trying to be first?

Everybody is talking. Rumors go around about one of your friends at school. You know the truth, but if you tell, you might get in trouble. Can you still stand up for what is right? What will you do?

Certain teens in your class are always made fun of. They get teased and pushed around, even by some of your friends. Are you going to stand up for this low-life—this nobody—or will you go along with the crowd? (Read James 2:1–4, 14–21.)

In biology class many of your friends tell the raunchiest jokes you have heard in ages. Sure, they got them from the latest video and the most-popular comic's routine. Everyone laughs at these stories and jokes that often take the Lord's name in vain. You've laughed before, but deep inside, you didn't like it. What will you do today? (Read Matthew 7:1, 2.)

Next ask yourself: *How far will I go to be a part of a certain group?* Maybe two of your friends are in a group. Where do you draw the line when it comes to copying a hair-style, or deciding what clothes you wear, the number of times you bathe, whether or not to use foul language, or to take drugs (or at least hang around places that will make people think you use drugs)? Being popular has a great cost. Ask yourself if you are willing to give up personal and godly respect to have the friendship of other people. In the long run feeling good about yourself deep inside is much more important than having kids hang around you because of what you wear, look like, and do on the outside.

Luke 15:6: "And when he finds it, he joyfully puts it on his shoulders and goes home. Then he calls his friends and neighbors together and says, 'Rejoice with me; I have found my lost sheep.' "

Can you share with your friends about the seemingly unimportant things that mean a lot to you—even though they don't seem newsworthy to everyone else? This will give you a good indication of who your true friends are. If they care about you, they will listen. They will laugh with you and hurt with you.

James 4:4 asks: ". . . Don't you know that friendship with the world is hatred toward God? Anyone who chooses to be a friend of the world becomes an enemy of God."

Today, take a look around and see who pays a high price in order to play the popularity game! Many times the "winners" are really "losers."

Recently a high-school sophomore sat beside me, with tears of hurt and pain in his eyes because he had played the popularity game. He shared that a friend had just died. The teen beside me had been his only Christian friend and because he wanted to stay popular, he had never shared Christ or the plan of salvation with him. Now his friend is dead, and he does not know where he spends eternity. That pain will last a lifetime.

If it's in your heart,
Speak out loud,
Don't just go along with the crowd!

26
Stop While You Can

She needed help. "I'm fifteen, and so is my boyfriend. We've been having sex on and off for about a year. My parents found out once, and they would kill me if they found out again. I know it's wrong, and I don't feel good about myself when I do it. We both know it makes God sad. I think my boyfriend would stop asking me to have sex, if I asked, but I'm afraid I'll lose him if I do."

What a perfect case of a girl knowing the right answer, but not acting on it! She knows it hurts her self-esteem and isn't the answer to keeping her boyfriend, but she hasn't the skills or courage to put a stop to it. Even though she realizes how much God hurts, she has more interest in herself than her long-term relationship with her boyfriend, God, or her parents. You see, the odds are great that her boyfriend will become history real soon. Boys don't stick around when they lose a challenge and their respect for a girl. Because she had sex with him, she will feel tremendous guilt and won't be able to look her parents in the eye. Is it worth a life of pain and lost friendships to have a few short moments' pleasure? Yes, you're really "built"—your mind, body and spirit. Hurt one part, and it affects all three.

Proverbs 14:12 warns, "There is a way that seems right to a man [woman], but in the end it leads to death."

The death that verse talks about includes self-esteem, friendships, and closeness to God. To avoid those consequences, you need God's Word as a blueprint for your life. Meditate on Romans 6:12–14.

Romans 6:13: Do not offer the parts of your body to sin, as instruments of wickedness, but rather offer yourself to God. . . .

27
Spare Change of Mind

Sue and Cherie were best friends until the day Sue saw Cherie with Sue's boyfriend. They were having a hamburger and talking, then they went for a ride. Sure, it looked bad, but it was purely innocent. That didn't matter, because Sue wouldn't change her mind; she would not be friends again. Some other friends told her not to give in, and she didn't. "How can I get her to change her mind?" Cherie asked. "I didn't even do anything!"

Has this ever happened to you? Because of a misunderstanding, someone you care very deeply about decides to do something and won't change her mind—absolutely stubborn.

Many parents and older people have never had someone who modeled forgiveness for them, so they easily become unreasonable and unyielding. Once it happened to me and sent me into a real depression. All I thought of at the time was suicide. I wasn't saved and was living a very worldly life, full of drugs and sin. Then a friend who had acted like my second father for several years thought I told him a lie. Twelve years have come and gone, and I don't know the exact facts. Maybe I did lie, and maybe I didn't. I have had to block all those painful memories from my mind. However, I will never forget how headstrong he was. Our friendship was over. He disowned me—forever—period!

I couldn't believe it. How could this be? Maybe this was a nightmare—but no, it was true. He meant it, and he wasn't about to change. Though I tried and tried to mend our friendship, he would accept nothing but the fact that his mind was firmly made up. Last time I saw him, twelve years ago, tears streaming down my face, I pleaded, and he shut the door in my face.

Life was over, I wanted to die. Instead I went home to my wife and cried profusely. She told me he wasn't worth it, but I wouldn't listen. Then she called my sister Mary, who talked sense into me. Mary told me neither he nor anyone else was worth taking my life. "God has great things for you. You're special and have great talents, Bill," she said. She went on and on. I cried and started the healing process that same day. I still thank God for placing my dear wife, Holly, and my sister, Mary, in the perfect spots that day.

Forgive and forget if you have to. Change your mind, if you were wrong. Sometimes things turn out okay when we are stubborn, but usually they don't. Read about a happy ending in Daniel 6:6–16. God saved Daniel in the end, but notice in verse 14 the king felt distressed but hadn't the courage to change his mind.

Now flip over to Mark 6:17–29. Notice in verse 26 how

John's words convicted and deeply distressed Herod, but he would not change his mind and save John's life—all because he made a stupid promise in front of his high-flying friends. If you must, let someone know you have changed your mind and heart toward him today.

People are always worth more than your pride.

28
Be Careful What You Study!

Across the country, we hear about teachers who have students do research on other religions besides Christianity. Students really get involved with one very scarey religion, when they do research and study it. Usually, however, their study earns them an A, so many will dig deeper and learn more about it.

A fourteen-year-old young man in New Jersey did a paper on Hinduism. But he became more interested in this religion the other kids were doing—the one almost guaranteed to earn him an A—Satanism. School officials and his fellow students say this boy became defiant and hostile while burying himself in library books on the occult and listening to heavy-metal rock music. Teachers noticed the difference, and on a Thursday, they warned his mother, but by Saturday night both mother and the son were dead. The son said he had a vision in which Satan came to him, wearing his own face, and urged him to kill his family. He preached Satanism. The boy stabbed his mother at least twelve times, and tried to kill his father and ten-year-old brother by setting fire to the house. Then he slit his own throat and wrist with a Boy Scout knife—and died in a pool of blood on the snow in a neighbor's backyard.

It is very dangerous to mess with the occult. For several years now I have spoken against the popular game Dungeons and Dragons, which gets participants to look deeper into the occult, to learn chants as well as other ways to get in touch with Satanic spirits. I urge you to get rid of any Ouija boards you or your friends have. Never mess with anything occult. If you listen to a band who prays to Satan, get rid of their albums. If you know any kids in school who play Dungeons and Dragons, get them help immediately by notifying someone who cares. You may save their lives.

The Bible instructs us to be naive in the things of the world, but Satan wants each one of us to commit suicide. He encourages us to make ourselves bigger than God.

Look at Isaiah 14:11–14, which describes Satan's fall:

All your pomp has been brought down to the grave, along with the noise of your harps; maggots are spread out beneath you and worms cover you. How you have fallen from heaven, O morning star, son of the dawn! You have been cast down to the earth, you who once laid low the nations! You said in your heart, "I will ascend to heaven; I will raise my throne above the stars of God; I will sit enthroned on the mount of assembly, on the utmost heights of the sacred mountain. I will ascend above the tops of the clouds; I will make myself like the Most High."

Notice how Satan uses the word *I*. He says, "*I* will ascend to heaven. *I* will raise my throne above the stars. *I* will sit on the mount. *I* will ascend above the heights. *I* will make myself like the Most High." Satan's entire game plan is to make us think someone could be greater than God, as when he was called in verse 12 "morning star." He tried to become greater than God, but he was cast out of heaven and into the pits of hell. When we mess with him, study him, and deal with anything that has to do with him—fortune-tellers, tarot cards, or anything that has to do with Satanism and the occult—that happens to us, too. It is very dangerous.

Whenever Satan challenges us, we can quote the words of Jesus in His confrontation with the devil:

Matthew 16:23: Jesus turned and said to Peter, "Out of my sight, Satan! You are a stumbling block to me; you do not have in mind the things of God, but the things of men."

Once again we can take the answer from God's book, when it comes to getting rid of Satan. James 4:7 says, "Submit yourselves, then, to God. Resist the devil, and he will flee from you." Hear the power in God's Word. The devil won't walk slowly away from you if you give yourself humbly to God; he will flee from you. *Flee* means "to run rapidly." Just say in faith, "In the name of Jesus Christ, I command you, Satan, to be gone."

29
Can't We Talk About It?

Dear Mom: I really feel as if you yell at me all the time. Why can't you just talk, instead of yelling and screaming?

When you are in a bad mood and I seem to make one little slipup, I really pay for it. You take out all your anger on me. Then I get so mad that we both get into a big fight. I don't think that is how a mother and daughter should get along, do you? I am just tired of all the fighting and yelling. I need you to be my mom—not a sister who is only worried about her own problems. Why can't we be friends . . . ?"

Many teenage girls could have written this letter from a daughter to her mother, because they feel that their mothers compete with them, or their mothers feel the girls are in competition with them. All moms today, especially single-parent mothers, have an incredible amount of pressure on their shoulders. Quite often when I share this competition dilemma with them, they confide that they feel their daughters have everything going for them, while the mothers work so hard with no appreciation and no thanks. If your mother got married at a young age, now that you are a teenager, she might only be in her thirties. She may feel she has missed out on some of the best years of her life because she had to raise you.

Encourage your mom not to feel that way by letting her know how much you love and appreciate her. It can make a world of difference in her life—and yours.

Romans 12:10: Be devoted to one another in brotherly love. Honor one another above yourselves.

30

What's Good About This?

Romans 8:28, "And we know that in all things God works for the good of those who love him, who have been called according to his purpose," is one of my favorite verses. When negative things happen in my life, such as suffering, hurt, pain, death, or sorrow, and I wonder what good can come of it, I turn to this passage.

Something happened in our house today that showed me the good that can come when things we don't understand happen. My little girl Emily has been in kindergarten three months. Each and every day my wife or I walked her to the bus stop, which is about eight houses away. The fact that it is around the corner, and you can't see our house from the bus stop, makes it especially scary for a little girl who is sensitive and intimidated by the larger, active, running and jumping boys four times her size. Today she was to walk by herself. Something that we didn't want to happen occurred yesterday. Emily got frightened at the last minute, when the other kids were getting on the bus. She became terrified and started screaming and crying, wanting us to take her home and drive her to school in the car. My wife held her ground. Even though the other kids were on the bus, she held Emily, and the bus driver came out, and they literally forced her into the bus. This had to stop.

The bus driver cleared out the front seat and put Emily there. She asked her who usually sat next to her. Then she called Ann (a nine-year-old neighbor) from the back of the bus to sit with Emily.

All day long my wife, Holly, could hardly enjoy a moment's peace, wondering about the ride there— wondering if she had done the right thing in forcing her through this so she could get over it and go beyond it. Emily came home from school, still sad. When she got into the house, she cried a little bit and told us she didn't want to get on the bus, and she wanted to ride in the car every day. We made our minds up and said that we couldn't take her to the bus stop anymore, and she had to walk there by herself. She's a kindergartener now, and she has to act like one. These are pretty big words for a short five-year-old girl.

Emily's friend Ann came over to play later that afternoon, so we asked if Emily could walk to the bus stop with her the next morning. Together we mapped out a plan: Emily would leave the house at 8:30 A.M. sharp, walk across our driveway, across our neighbors' yard, up Ann's driveway, go to the door, and there would be Ann at the door at 8:31 A.M. It was all set. That night, we could hardly sleep. It was kind of like a NASA takeoff. We watched the clock the next morning: 8:28 . . . 8:29. Boots on, hat on, leg warmers on . . . 8:30 A.M. Out the door. *You can do it, Emily.* Holly and I, along with Emily's brother and sister, anxiously waited at the door as she walked away without turning back. We said, "Let's shut the door. We don't want her to see us watching her." So we shut the door and peeked through the window. She walked down our driveway, across the neighbors' yard, up Ann's driveway, and stopped suddenly. She turned around and started heading back. Because we had not planned on this, we didn't know what to do. She was coming back, crying like a baby. What could we do? I went to the door, and like a caring, concerned father, I called out, "What are you doing?" She was still crying. I yelled, "Go to Ann's house."

"She's not out here," Emily answered. "I told you she wouldn't come."

"I think I hear her door opening now." I prayed, *Lord, can't You at least open that door?* Lo and behold, guess what? Ann appeared behind Emily, walking toward her. Emily wiped her tears, Ann took her hand, and they walked off toward the bus stop. That afternoon Emily came home as proud as a third grader. (As far as Emily is concerned, *nothing* could be better than being a third grader.)

Perhaps you find it hard to understand how a child could feel so afraid of getting on the schoolbus, but remember when you were in kindergarten and first grade. What scared you? Handling fears today is no different from when you were a child. Each of us has to face up to them.

We have to walk through our fears and realize that no matter what happens to us, God gave us choices. We can act so that we can see, find, and really believe in the good behind our situations.

1 Thessalonians 5:16–18 (italics added):   Be joyful always; pray continually; *give thanks in all circumstances*, for this is God's will for you in Christ Jesus.

When we're pushed over the line, many times we win the race.

31
I'll Take Care of You

He was about twenty years old, with a worried look on his face and tattoos on his arm. As I left the assembly early that morning, this young man who looked too old to be in high school said, "I need to talk to you. When can we talk? Please . . . I need some help."

I was being rushed from the high school to the junior high a few miles away, so I said, "Can we meet at lunch?"

"Okay, I'll try."

I didn't see him until that evening, before I spoke to the parents, when I saw him waiting for me. We didn't have time to talk beforehand, but he promised to be there afterwards. We both anxiously waited: me to help, and him to learn. From the look on his face, I knew he didn't want to talk to me about how he planned to face his bright future.

After the evening session I was signing autographs in my books and telling people what the tapes contained, and so on. When I had gotten only about halfway done with the books and tapes, he appeared. "Let's talk now. We have a few moments," I invited him.

We sat down at a table, and before I knew it he unfolded his story. He was about to go into the army, and his future didn't seem bright. He had very little to live for. Did he know what it meant to have total peace in his heart and to know where he was going, why he lived, and what he was all about? I asked. He said, "No," then wondered, "What do you have that I don't have?" Whenever I hear that question, I know people need more than just positive thinking, more than just a few clichés, fancy words, or charming sentences. I knew he needed truth; he needed what gives me the hope of a lifetime, courage to handle each new day. He needed to have in his heart what I had in mine.

I shared the gospel with him: how Jesus loved us so much that He gave up His own life so we could have eternal life, died, was buried, went into hell and rose again so we would never have to go to hell. He paid the price for us! We must be sorry, I told him, and ask God to be our Lord and Savior and try to truly live for Him. That young man understood it all. He had been ready for a long time. I am sure other people had shared with him, because that evening, while we sat at the table, it was as though a glass jar had been placed around us. He prayed with me and asked Christ to come into his heart. He cried for his sins, he hurt, and I knew it was genuine. Within the next few minutes, we hugged and laughed together. I shared how he would be spending eternity with me in heaven someday. I got his address and I was going to send him some more materials. When we looked up, we realized we were alone in the entire cafeteria. Because people had sensed we had a special moment going, they gave us the freedom and space to share. The principal or superintendent (I can't remember which) came over to me and said, "That was a wonderful thing that you just did with that young man. I heard your conversation. I want you to know that we are going to keep the rest of these books and tapes for the school, and I will send you a check next week."

As I drove home, it was as though God was saying, "If you take care of My business, I will take care of you and your business." Because I stood up for God and was more interested in having a new Christian brother that evening than selling all the books and tapes in the world, I knew the joy of seeing another person come to the Lord. (That is the only time, by the way, that the angels jump in heaven and sing and shout—when a new Christian is born—when a sinner turns from Satan to the Lord.)

I have also seen that money, fame and popularity mean nothing when you are home alone at night, when you hurt inside because you have tried to keep a step ahead of everyone else and to be a big shot—and you've failed. I am just thankful that God touched my heart and wanted me to have another brother in heaven.

If you stand up for God, He will take care of you. If you memorize Scripture, he will make it easier for you to memorize your homework and your studies. Share Christ with a hurting person in school or at your job. God will give you a piece of happiness you can't describe any other way—you can't pay for it, you can't buy it, you can't find it—only God has it, and it is *free*. He wants to give it to you today. Let Him take care of you as He did me that wonderful night. If you haven't received this free gift from God—take it! If you've already "taken it," then "pass it along"!

Matthew 6:33: "But seek first his kingdom and his righteousness, and all these things will be given to you as well."

Matthew 10:32, 33: "Whoever acknowledges me before men, I will also acknowledge him before my Father in heaven. But whoever disowns me before men, I will disown him before my Father in heaven."

32
What's *Bonding?*

My boyfriend and I have been going together for three years. We've had sex many times. While we both feel somewhat bad about it, we plan to get married. My question is: We are still attracted to each other the way we were when we first met, but we don't feel real close inside. Can you tell me why?

Though this is a problem that could have many possible solutions, I've just learned a fascinating concept that might give you some answers. The following steps lead to proper bonding, where one spirit and one person become attached to another.

Only if you have been very fortunate and read a great deal, would you have come across these ideas. I've never been taught them in school or a seminar. I believe many marriages would have lasted had the couples not skipped several (or most) of these steps.

One-night stands devastate relationships because 70 to 80 percent of these steps are completely skipped over. Also, many marriages fail because husbands and wives forget to go through each step and spend the proper amount of time on one before they move to the next. I really believe that your boyfriend and you, having had sex many times, were probably attracted and drawn close because of physical attraction, and your hormones got the best of you. Here are the progressive bonding steps, described in *Bonding: Relationships in the Image of God*, by Donald M. Joy, and *The Tangled Wing: Biological Constraints on the Human Spirit*, by Melvin Konner:

1. Eye to body—Noticing each other.
2. Eye to eye—Feeling a bit embarrassed and reserved.
3. Voice to voice—Spending 100 hours on the phone.
4. Hand to hand—Not necessarily holding hands, but standing side by side, heading in the same direction.
5. Arm to shoulder—As buddies.
6. Arm to waist—Sharing secrets, picture a couple "talking in a bucket."
7. Face to face—Gazing into each other's eyes, includes intimate kissing.
8. Hand to head—Stroking face or hair while talking or kissing—shows trust level.
9. Hand to body (not sexual)—Another type of "eye to body,"—accepting the imperfections in each other's body.
10. Mouth to breast—Not practiced by any other species, shows tenderness and helplessness in the male.
11. Hand to genitals.
12. Intercourse.

It is vital that you realize *the last three steps are only to be done after marriage (see Genesis 2:24).*

Notice how most guy-girl attractions easily take into account the first four or five steps. The problem is that when they totally focus on sex, they do not spend the proper amount of time in each step. People often rush over them because:

1. They think totally of themselves and their desires.
2. They lack respect for the other person, as well as God and His rules.

In a properly bonded marriage, the first eleven steps happen almost daily. Going through them can also rebuild love, when a marriage is in trouble, hurting, or the feelings are gone.

God has His ways: They are called right. We can be right or wrong. Listen to these wise outtakes from God's Word:

Hosea 14:9: Who is wise? He will realize these things. Who is discerning? He will understand them. The ways of the Lord are right; the righteous walk in them, but the rebellious stumble in them.

We have a choice: Walking or stumbling, obedience or rebellion.

Isaiah 55:8, 9: "For my thoughts are not your thoughts, neither are your ways my ways," declares the Lord. "As the heavens are higher than the earth, so are my ways higher than your ways and my thoughts than your thoughts."

Let God have His way today.

33

It's the Little Things

Hundreds of times each year, I counsel teenagers through the mail.

A few months ago I got a letter from a deeply troubled, depressed girl, who had little to live for and very little hope for the future. I counseled her the best I could through practical steps from my book *Tough Turf*; I gave her many Bible verses full of hope and encouragement and offered her an ongoing relationship through the mail, for as long as it would take to help her get back on her feet emotionally, spiritually, and mentally.

I received another letter from her, a short time later, with the same attitudes and despondency. Nothing I said seemed to have clicked. She could not see herself doing or believe in anything I had offered her.

I have a friend named Arla, a very caring person who also writes to many of the people I write to. I gave the letter to Arla and asked her to try to reach this girl, since nothing I did seemed to work. Arla wrote a letter filled with Scripture, hope, and practical steps. When the girl wrote back, she sent Arla a picture. Even when she replied to Arla's letter, she still seemed the same—without hope, hurting, full of pain, and nowhere to turn. As Arla wrote back the second time, she again applied the same principles we always do: meet people where they are, listen to them, give them real help and encouragement by way of God's Word and practical steps, and pray for God to work in their hearts. Along with all this, Arla also mentioned that she enjoyed receiving her picture and said, "Your eyes are really beautiful." Just a few days later Arla received a third letter; this time the girl's attitude was completely changed. Now she focused on the future, not the past, had applied some of the Scriptures Arla had shared, and was digging into her Bible and making God a real part of her life. We believe that she is very close to accepting Jesus as her personal Savior. Arla's sentence mentioning how lovely her eyes were grabbed ahold of the hopeless teen. In her letter she shared that no one had ever said anything like that before. She had read that sentence over and over and started to apply Scripture to her life, and realized she has a lot of good going for her and a bright future ahead, if she will work hard and do certain things.

Isn't it amazing what a tiny compliment can do? One smile can start a friendship. A dose of laughter can cause someone's pain to go away. A little hope can get someone to look toward the future, not the past. Love can rebuild an entire family.

A couple of days ago, my family and I went to a restaurant. When we arrived, all the waitresses were busy, and it looked as if we would have quite a wait. We sat an extra five or ten minutes before they even took our order, but the little courtesies and the smile the waitress gave us made it all okay. I had thought about being angry and not enjoying my breakfast as much, until she showed she cared—even just a little bit.

What little thing can you do today for someone to pick up her spirits, to give him renewed vision or hope? Remember: The little things make a big difference.

One young girl sent me a letter; first she told me her parents didn't understand her, and because she is older, they expect so much more from her than from her younger brother. It was really a cry for help. Her last statement to her parents went like this, "I love you two so much that it is very easy to get angry at you. I know that doesn't make much sense right now, but it will. Just give me a little bit more patience, love, caring, and attention. Just a little more is all that I ask."

I believe this teenager speaks for all of us, when we ask our friends, classmates, and family members to just notice us a little bit more.

Proverbs 12:25:   An anxious heart weighs a man down, but a kind word cheers him up.

Say that kind word to someone today, and remember not to go alone. Take God with you, wherever you go.

34
Do I Have to Move?

Every year thousands of families have to move. Job relocations, plant closings, a better territory, a broken family—there are hundreds of reasons. Many times teenagers get caught up in the shuffle.

When I was a sixteen-year-old sophomore, my father relocated to another town, which meant we had to move. I had gone to a very small high school, where I felt really comfortable. The school I moved to was ten times as large, with a thousand more kids. *What did I do wrong that caused us to move,* I wondered, until my dad told me it was scary, but he wanted to move because the opportunities ahead would be better for all of us. My family moved in the middle of the summer, but not me. To finish driver's training, I stayed with a friend, and I wanted to remain there through my junior and senior year. I just couldn't imagine moving away from my hometown, my roots, my comfort zone. I felt afraid, expected the worst, and imagined every kind of fearful thing. But nothing awful happened. The worst event I experienced was taking two and a half weeks to find my new locker. (Many people say that I am exaggerating, but I am not at all.) I knew one fellow when I moved there. We rode the bus together in the morning and took it home together at night. Because all the kids, all the rooms, the different floors, and so on overwhelmed me, I kept my books with him and didn't even worry about finding my locker until the third week of the school year. By then my friend had gotten sick and tired of my taking up all his space.

If you have to move, think of the new opportunities and friends it will provide. Yes, you feel sad about leaving old friends behind, and it is scary to make a change, but life is full of changes. Only when we change do we grow. If we stay the same we get stagnant.

As I look back, I can clearly see that outside of my family, the major things that shaped my life happened because of that move. The jobs I took in my new town helped me grow and expand far beyond anything available where I used to live. Several key people who have influenced my life greatly only came into my life after that move. College, traveling through the United States, painting parking lines with my friend Steve, and many more opportunities opened to me because of the different geographical area we moved to. By the way, my dad was in his fifties, and the move definitely frightened him as well. He moved, earning no more pay, but because he moved, just ten years later his retirement benefits were forty times greater than they would have been had he stayed in the little shop where he worked for over thirty years.

Yes, it can be scary to move, but it is just like life . . . if we don't move, we stay in the same place. Kind of like coasting . . . sometimes you feel you are doing a good job and you can just coast along. You have worked hard at your studies, but now you plan to rest and take it easy. Remember, you can only coast downhill. You can't even do it on flat ground for very long, or you will stop. Then if you don't get going again, you will not be able to improve or grow at all. Coasting takes the momentum you build up by going down the hill.

If you or a friend have a move in your future, make the

best of it. *Look ahead.* Don't concentrate on what you are losing or leaving behind. Get excited about the new opportunities and people waiting for you.

Proverbs 3:5, 6: Trust in the Lord with all your heart and lean not on your own understanding; in all your ways acknowledge him, and he will make your paths straight.

35

"Everyone Else Is"

I have a problem with my parents. They don't care what I do. They say I can do anything and go anywhere, just as long as I don't get into trouble. My grades are suffering, and I need some guidelines. Help!

Can you imagine feeling like this—upset because your parents are giving you too much freedom? Many teens say, "Try me, try me"—except for the ones who have parents, like the girl who wrote this letter, who won't say no.

In my talks I tell young people they are very fortunate if they have parents who love them enough and have a strong enough relationship with them to say no. Most teens in the audience roll their eyes when I say this, but not the ones who have to make decisions all alone.

We all need a pilot in life. When we drive over a tall

bridge, if we can see guard rails on each side, we feel more secure. We won't go close to them, but it feels good just having them there. Studies also show that in a divorce situation teens and preteens would rather live with the parent who is the firmest disciplinarian, with defined rules to follow. You might say they're looking for a pilot.

Are you one of the lucky ones? Do your parents say no? Do they explain why they are against this or that? If He meant you to go through these early years on your own, God wouldn't have given you parents.

What is known as the first commandment with a promise, and what is that promise? Look it up and find out. It's somewhere between Deuteronomy 5:6–16. Here's a hint! It's the fifth commandment. Notice God's specific promise to you.

Paul puts "disobeying parents" next to God haters and murderers in Romans 1:30, 31. If your parents are trying their best to train you for a life on your own, you may want to tell them, "Thanks for saying no."

Ephesians 6:1–4: Children, obey your parents in the Lord, for this is right. "Honor your father and mother"—which is the first commandment with a promise—"that it may go well with you and that you may enjoy long life on the earth."

Fathers, do not exasperate your children; instead, bring them up in the training and instruction of the Lord.

36

It Takes Courage

Her name is Nikki Lemieux, and I close each and every one of my assembly talks with her story. Over the last eight years, approximately 500,000 people have heard and been encouraged by her example.

Nikki is a neighbor of mine and one of the most bubbly and exciting people you will ever know. In seventh grade she found out that she had leukemia. Because of the treatments, a short time later she lost her long, wavy hair that used to reach clear down her back. She conformed and wore a wig. The kids were brutal, however, and the first three weeks of eighth grade were the roughest time for her. Her wig was pulled off enough times to hurt so deeply that she thought she would never go back to school.

What happened the next Monday morning, just three weeks into the eighth grade, has taught so many about the beautiful word *courage*. As she was about to get out of the car and walk across a parking lot filled with six hundred kids, she said to her mom and dad, "Guess what I am going to do today?"

"What, honey?"

"Today I am going to find out who my real friends are." With that she pulled off her wig and set it on the seat beside her. Her mom and dad sat there, with tears flowing down their faces. Nikki said, "Pray hard, Mom and Dad. I know that the Lord is walking with me, and I know you will be there, too." She said it was the toughest walk she ever had to make, not knowing what lay ahead.

Knowing Nikki as I do, I believe that as she walked away from that car, all scared and afraid of what might happen, she was also concerned about her mom and dad, hurting in the car. I can just imagine her saying a prayer that their pain would be eased just a bit as she walked into school. The kids just stood and stared. For the following days and weeks, they were nothing but supportive. They truly admired her courage.

Her disease is now in remission. She went on to high school, graduated with a 3.8 GPA, and has gone to college in Canada. In high school she won the two most prestigious awards given by students and faculty alike. Today she counsels with other kids at her school and in her dorm.

I can't tell you how many teenagers across this country have written to me, saying that if Nikki could do it with God's help, so could they. A local magazine just recorded the entire story, and as I read it I couldn't help but cry the whole way through. Nikki said she can't believe that some young people feel they have nothing to do and just lie around and watch TV. She says there is so much to do, so many things to experience, and she wishes she could get by with only two hours of sleep so she could learn more of what God has to offer in this beautiful thing called life.

On the wall in Nikki's home is a plaque that reads:

I'm an old man now.
I've seen a lot of trouble.
Most of it never happened.

Then there is Nikki's own personal motto: "Learn as if you were to live forever; live as if you were to die tomorrow."

Nikki has taught me a great deal about life, faith, and not being afraid to hug and kiss a family member, no matter where you might be. Never be ashamed to tell someone, "I love you." Nikki says, "I realized that I had to start appreciating things a lot more, because I might not be around as long as I thought I would. You begin to live one day at a time, because it could be your last."

Today I challenge you to find out who your real friends are! If you are wise, like Nikki, you will realize that some of them are your family members, and you won't be ashamed to hug, kiss, or say "I love you" anytime or anywhere. It will be a privilege to bring friends home to meet the family that you are proud of.

Take a moment and read Psalms 1:1–3. Notice that God will bless us if we don't hang around certain people, if we don't take advice from certain people, and if we don't continually associate with people who don't love Him.

If you want to know the secret of making new friends, remember my paraphrase of Matthew 7:12: "However you want people to treat you, so treat them, for this is the law and the prophets."

Take Nikki with you today. If you need extra courage in some area of your life, remember how she took off her wig, and physically reach up over your head and take off a layer of fear from your body. Look to God, as she did to her parents that morning, and say, "I know You're with me. Together we can make it through this." Have a super day!

37
What Kind
of Love Is This?

Phil Driscoll sings a song about the kind of love Jesus must have had to give up his life for his friends. I've listened to this song over and over again; I love the music and Phil's style of singing. However, I had heard the song many times before I asked myself: *What types of love are there?*

Everywhere we turn, look, and listen, we hear about love. Many people think that love is the same as romance. Some think that love means having sex. Lots of people don't know love, because they have had the wrong kind of love. Many feel skeptical when others say, "I love you," because they don't know what they want in return.

Do you have some hangups, fears, or concerns about love? I hope so. This subject affects all of us. Listen to the songs on the radio, and you'll notice nine out of ten will be about love. Most of the time secular music talks about a very selfish love. The songs say, "I want you," "I want you to do this for me," "I need you," and so on. For the next few days let's look at God's Word and see what He says about love. We can start with the most popular verse in the entire Bible:

John 3:16: "For God so loved the world that he gave his one and only Son, that whoever believes in him shall not perish but have eternal life."

Never fear what God's love did for us: It sent His Son to us, made Jesus sin for us, and gave us the opportunity to have everlasting life. God's love did a wonderful and powerful thing for us.

When you think about human love, ask what that love is doing for you and the other person. Is it a selfish love or a giving, sharing, and concerned love?

Take a few minutes now to look up John 15:12, 13. Read these verses and ask yourself: *Does God ask us to love each other as He loved us, or does He command us to?* Right, it is a command. When Phil Driscoll's song asks about the love that willingly sacrifices a life for friends, verse 13 tells us it is the greatest love of all.

"Greater love has no one than this, that one lay down his life for his friends" (v. 13). I love the sound of that verse. God's love and the kind of love He wants us to give others shows not only in words, but in deeds. God's love was His sacrificial death. When we do things for other people, we truly show our love.

My wife and I have a standing joke. We will be sitting at the table, and one of us will mention that he or she would like to have a glass of pop, for instance. Each really waits for the other person to get up, but neither of us gets up to get it. As soon as one gets up, the sitting person says, "I'll get it." By then it is too late, because the other has already gone. It is easy to say, "I'll get it," when you know you don't have to expend the energy to do it. True love means going out of your way to help other people. Christ did not have to brag about washing the disciples' feet. He just washed them.

38
The Love
of a Pure Heart

First Timothy 1:5 describes three key elements of love: "The goal of this command is love, which comes from a pure heart and a good conscience and a sincere faith." What are they? A pure heart, a good conscience, and a sincere faith.

Anyone with a truly pure heart would not want to abuse your body by having sex with you, nor would you have it with anyone else.

Also, if you and your boyfriend have good consciences, you can live with yourselves before the date, during the date, and after the date. Once she became a born-again Christian, a friend's daughter began asking her boyfriend to pray with her before they left for a date. They asked God for safety and a fun, enjoyable time. "You wouldn't believe how nicely my boyfriend is treating me these days, especially since he knows we are going to be praying again at the end of the date," she told her dad. That is what a good conscience is all about.

I believe a good conscience comes from a sincere faith. To have faith in God and not to put it to work, to me means that it might not be sincere. If we have a sincere faith, love for Christ and want to represent God and all that He stands for, we will uphold His image in everything we do, even when it gets dark, even behind closed doors, even when two of us are alone and our hearts pump at five times the normal rate. Wind yourself up tight for God, and the world won't unravel you.

39
Sincere Love

Romans 12:9 talks about it this way: "Love must be sincere. Hate what is evil; cling to what is good." Do you know what it means to hate what is evil? It means to hate Satan. The same Satan who tries to get us to go too far on a date murders, rapes, and abuses children. He cares not how much alcohol or drugs we put into our systems. This Satan wanted to be equal with God and started all humanity on a course bound up in sin. His ultimate goal is for you and every one of your friends to commit suicide. If he can't do that, he wants you to live a life of depression, anger, bitterness, and worry.

We are to hate what is evil and cling to the Lord. Cling to what is good. If we don't hide God's Word in our hearts and we get into a passionate moment, we will have nothing to hang onto, except our feelings of the moment. God's Word is like superglue—we should be stuck on it forever.

Please read Mark 10:17–21, about the rich young man. He wanted to know how to get to heaven. He said he never broke any of God's laws, but he had a problem. His heart and his love were in the wrong place. It says in verse 21, "Jesus felt genuine love for this man as he looked at him. 'You lack only one thing,' he told him; 'go and sell all you have and give the money to the poor—and you shall have treasure in heaven—and come, follow me'" (TLB).

Notice Jesus had genuine love for this man. That's why he could offer tough yet needed advice to his friend. Please realize that Jesus isn't asking His followers to sell all they have. He merely wants to know where our hearts are and where our sincere love is. He knew He might lose this man as a follower, but He gave the best advice He knew, because He wanted the best for His friend, and not necessarily Himself.

Is your love toward your friends sincere? Can you offer advice that is hard to give? Do you continue doing things and going places with your friends, even if you know you are hurting your parents, God, and yourself? Sincere love isn't easy, but it sure is beautiful!

40
Serving Love

Galatians 5:13:   You, my brothers, were called to be free. But do not use your freedom to indulge the sinful nature; rather, serve one another in love.

We are free from sin and called to be free and serve. Look at that word *serve*. If we serve one another, we look for ways in which we can truly help other people, meet their needs, especially when we get no applause or recognition. That is freedom, freedom from others' approval, acceptance, and applause. That is love.

Since we are free, Paul cautions us, very simply, not to use the freedom to indulge our sinful nature. We should never use compassion and friendship to cause someone else to sin. If we tune in to a secular station, the words of the songs on the radio don't honor God. These people care not about God's ways. They want to do what feels good as often as they wish, because their main goal in life is to please themselves, to be happy, and to have fun.

Our goal is different. In serving one another we truly become the kind of lovers God wants us to be. Go back over the verses from the last three days before you close the book for today. Ask God how He wants you to fall back in love with your parents, your brothers and sisters, and your close friends. It is a beautiful way of life, and we don't have to worry about being knocked off the charts, like many of those other love songs, week in and week out. God's way is wonderful, and it lasts forever. Yes, if God sent you a love letter, He'd sign it "forever yours."

41
Save a Life . . . Stop a Suicide

If one of your friends threatened to commit suicide, would you act as if he'd made a joke? Would you laugh it off or would you know how to help her? Do you know what signs to look for? Don't just say that it only happens to other people. Today suicide is the second-biggest killer of young people between the ages of fifteen and twenty-four. Each one of us knows of a family in which a person has taken his or her own life.

According to the American Association of Suicidology, five distinct warning signs should automatically alert us to a potential suicide:

1. *A suicide threat or other statement indicating a desire or intention to die.* If you ever hear one of your friends say, "I

can't take this pressure anymore," "Life isn't worth it," "The stress is too great," or, "I just can't take it," don't take these threats idly! Take them for real. Notice when your friend has his head slumped and is acting different—especially standing by the locker, walking down the hall, or in the cafeteria.

2. *A previous suicide attempt.* I recently heard a woman tell about a student who tried to erase herself to death. That's right—rubbing an eraser on each wrist. No one noticed it in class. After she tried an eraser, rubbing it back and forth over and over again, she turned to a paper clip—rubbing it over and over on her skin. No one noticed, so she turned to glass and finally to a razor blade. Please keep your eye out for other kids and loved ones who have mentioned a previous suicide attempt or who are doing things indicating that.

3. *Mental depression.* There is a lot of stress for young people today—and for parents as well. Juniors and seniors constantly talk to me about the amount of stress, keeping their grades up, what school to go to, what to do after high school or college, how to put up with what everyone expects them to do, and so on. The only way to deal with this kind of stress is to develop coping skills. Talk to your friends. Pump iron or exercise. If you like to be alone, be alone, or if you like to be with other people, then be with them. If music helps you enjoy yourself and forget your pressures, then try it. Just remember—don't try to cope with depression through things that add to the depression. Alcohol and drugs only add to the long-term depression. Cope in a positive way.

4. *Marked changes in personality or behavior.* As a friend you will notice "mood swings" before anyone else. You are around that person more than anyone else, and you can tell when he or she changes.

5. *Making arrangements, as though for a final departure.* When other students start giving away things such as jewelry, pets, a record collection, and so on, *beware!*

(Especially if that person is in a good mood.) If you've noticed that someone has been bummed out for two or three weeks and then becomes high, happy, smiling, and starts giving things away, this is a very important warning sign—maybe the most important of all—for you to notice. Your friend seems happy because she has an inner peace; she has made the decision to kill herself. In her mind she thinks she's found the right answer.

What do you do if you recognize these signs in a friend? Follow these steps:

1. *Discuss the topic of suicide openly and frankly. Do not be afraid to use the word* suicide *in your discussion.* Remember, you are a friend and not a counselor, but you can help. Don't be fake, be genuine. Others have laughed at your friend and said, "You won't do it," "You'll never carry it through," or, "You're just talking about it." Don't make the same mistake!

2. *Show interest and support.* Be honest. Don't just try to get that person through the first hour, second hour, and third hour. Give him positive reinforcement. Let him know you really care. If you see he is doing something fantastic or positive, tell him about it. Be a genuine friend. Honesty and sincerity are vitally important here. If he doesn't see that you show interest and give support, he will probably feel you are just like his parents (who may be ignoring him and too busy for him) or like other friends who have not picked up on the signals. Please, be interested and show support. One of the best things you can say is, "I really care about you, and I want to do what I can to help," or, "You are my friend. I don't want to lose my friend. I want you here with me. I care about you, and I am going to be here to help . . . no matter what or how long it takes."

3. *Get professional help!* Tell somebody you believe can help, someone you can trust. *Don't* keep this a secret. You've got to get professional help: a teacher, a counselor, or an adult

trained in this, who can talk to your friend. Even if your friend looks you in the eye and says, "I'll hate you the rest of my life, if you tell anyone," it doesn't matter. You must get professional help. Continually tell her you care, and that is the reason you are doing this. I guarantee you that she will come back later—maybe many weeks or months later—and thank you for being there, holding strong, and doing what was right. She might feel angry and hate you, but keep telling her that you are doing it because you do care about her

After one senior took his own life, others found out what had happened before the suicide. He told all eight of his friends how he was going to kill himself, when he was going to do it, and even why. All eight ignored it. They all tried to hide it, and each one told him to his face that he would not carry it out—but he did! Now they have lost a friend, and all of them feel angry with themselves and him, but they are also frustrated and very guilty. They will have to carry that scar for the rest of their lives.

People are too important and life is too precious for us to let caring go by the wayside, for us not to pick up warning signs and not have steps to follow when someone hurts. Encourage others to read this chapter, too, and know the signs.

Find the suicide crisis line in your area. You can call it anytime. Help someone who hurts. Most of all, *care*. Then know what to do. With God as your helper, you will have the strength to notice and follow through with the help that is needed to save a life.

When someone feels heavy under the burdens and pressures of stress, depression, or hopelessness, give him the ultimate gift: Jesus Christ. He makes a plea to your hurting friend and to you when you are down and out:

Matthew 11:28–30: "Come to me, all you who are weary and burdened, and I will give you rest. Take my yoke upon you and learn from me, for I am gentle and humble in heart, and you will find rest for your souls. For my yoke is easy and my burden is light."

42
Open Heart, Open Home

What would you do if you were driving along the Chicago River, near Chicago, Illinois, and you saw a shack made of rotten wood, sheet metal, and canvas? The day was freezing cold, sub-zero weather, with a windchill even worse. What would you do if you saw two men in their thirties beside the shack—bums, dirty, cold—and you did not know if they were winos. Both of them huddled by a fire with their clothes, which didn't fit at all, piled on layer by layer.

If you were like me, you probably would have felt sorry for them but driven right by. That's not what a couple from New Mexico did, however. They went home, contacted a newspaper, and said that if they could get ahold of the man who lived in the shack (who turned out to be Harold Thomas), they would send him a bus ticket, and provide him with a job, working on their farm in New Mexico. The man replied, "I'm willing to give it a shot. This is an opportunity, and I'm going to take it. Opportunities don't knock but once."

Wow! When I read that story, I couldn't help but think about the people I pass by every day and never stop to give a hand. I feel sorry for them or say a prayer, but I keep on going. Here are three verses that will help each one of us be a little closer to the example God wants us to be in our lives here on earth.

Isaiah 58:7: "Is it not to share your food with the hungry and to provide the poor wanderer with shelter—when you see the naked, to clothe him, and not to turn away from your own flesh and blood?"

1 Timothy 6:18, 19: Command them to do good, to be rich in good deeds, and to be generous and willing to share. In this way they will lay up treasure for themselves as a firm foundation for the coming age, so that they may take hold of the life that is truly life.

Hebrews 13:16: And do not forget to do good and to share with others, for with such sacrifices God is pleased.

43
Short People

About ten years ago a song entitled "Short People" put them down. It even claimed they had no reason to live.

My little girl, Emily, is the smallest student in the entire elementary school. She is in kindergarten, and she is smaller than anyone there. Her self-esteem will depend on how people act toward her and how she reacts. If they call her names, she will find it very difficult to accept and put up with.

We usually call people names and use put-downs when they are different. I asked Emily about two neighbor girls who are black. I said, "Are they different?"

She said, "Yes."

"Are they bad?"

"No. They are neat people, Daddy. I really like them." We found out that different is just different. It is not bad, scary, or frightening; we need not talk down or get angry at something just because it's different. We can choose to wallow in our differences or to make the best of them and be creative.

A very short man in the Bible had a goal he didn't think he could ever reach. Zacchaeus wanted to see Jesus. What did he do? The people were too tall and the crowds were too thick, so he climbed a tree. That is creativity. As Jesus passed by, He looked up and said, "Come on down." Guess what? Zacchaeus jumped on down. Of course, many people didn't like it (like the Pharisees, who nagged, yelled and put down the shorter man), but Jesus didn't mind. He knows that different is only different, not bad, because He created different. Christ's purpose on earth was to meet our needs, save us from our sins, no matter if we are tall or short, black or white, introvert or extrovert, good or bad. He came to save all of us who are sick in sin.

Watch out for put-downs. If you are short, think of Zacchaeus. Look up, and you won't be short at all.

Luke 19:1–10: Jesus entered Jericho and was passing through. A man was there by the name of Zacchaeus; he was a chief tax collector and was wealthy. He wanted to see who Jesus was, but being a short man he could not, because of the crowd. So he ran ahead and climbed a sycamore-fig tree to see him, since Jesus was coming that way.

When Jesus reached the spot, he looked up and said to him, "Zacchaeus, come down immediately. I must stay at your house today." So he came down at once and welcomed him gladly.

All the people saw this and began to mutter, "He has gone to be the guest of a 'sinner.'"

But Zacchaeus stood up and said to the Lord, "Look, Lord! Here and now I give half of my possessions to the poor, and if I have cheated anybody out of anything, I will pay back four times the amount." Jesus said to him, "Today salvation has come to this house, because this man, too, is a son of Abraham. For the Son of Man came to seek and to save what was lost."

By the way, I'm teaching Emily how to climb trees.

44

They Warned Her

Recently a tragedy occurred at our local university. A student went jogging one night and was sexually assaulted and strangled; they found her nude body the next morning. As I read the newspaper account, I could hardly believe the comments her family and friends made about the incident.

Many times, they said, they had warned her about jogging alone at night. She was independent and strong willed, as well as a wonderful person, and never listened to their warnings.

How inconsiderate, to tell the newspaper about the warnings, instead of merely concentrating on their love for her at this time of grief and heartache, I thought. As I put down the newspaper I realized they shared those warnings when she was alive, because they loved her, and even now they shared the same warnings because they loved other people.

God's book is full of warnings. When I was younger, I thought Christianity was just a bunch of *dos* and *don'ts*—mostly *don'ts*. It seems as if all the things Christians could do weren't any fun. But I have come to realize—especially after working with so many hurting teens and parents—that God loves us so much that He gives us guidelines. He cares for us so deeply that He puts rails on the tall bridges of life, so we won't fear falling, so we can look straight ahead.

Think of some of the warnings your parents and other concerned people in society have given you. *Don't drink and drive.* Why would anyone say that? First, maybe they want you to stay alive. Second, they hope that if they were part of an innocent family driving toward you late at night and you swerved, they and their children wouldn't have to die, all because a young person didn't listen to a loved one's warning.

Put on your seat belt. In many states it's the law. Buckle up. Many teenagers don't have the courage to put their seat belts on in the same car as other teens who do not wear theirs. Call it peer pressure, lack of will, or being a coward. Usually it's because we don't truly take to heart the warning that seat belts can save lives. We've heard about one person who lived because she was thrown from the car, but the facts truly show that you are twenty-five times more likely to live through a car accident if you wear your seat belt.

My friend John Crudele asks his audience if they have ever seen a flat, brown, furry pancake in the road—it used to be a squirrel. That squirrel ended up there because it didn't listen to its mother's warning when she said, "Stay out of the road." Life has many such tragic endings if we don't follow certain warnings.

God has given us a few spiritual warnings. Look at Proverbs 23:17: "Do not let your heart envy sinners, but always be zealous for the fear of the Lord." As His young person, God is telling you "Don't envy the parties at your school or those who keep telling about their wild experiences with the opposite sex." Get excited about your love and respect (the Bible calls it fear) for God.

Proverbs 16:20 promises: "Whoever gives heed to instruction prospers, and blessed is he who trusts in the Lord." If you want to be blessed and have good things happen to you, *listen* when someone gives you advice. God speaks through your parents, pastor, books like this, and other people who really care about you. Look what God calls us if we don't listen to His helpful warnings and advice. "A *mocker* resents correction; he will not consult the wise" (Proverbs 15:12, *italics mine*). "A *fool* spurns his father's discipline, but whoever heeds correction shows prudence [wisdom, foresight, coolness]" (Proverbs 15:5, *italics mine*).

Remember that people can show love in many ways, and it's not always true love when someone lets you wander aimlessly and freely through life, with no guidelines and no warnings. Today think of some of the things your parents, teachers, and truly concerned friends have warned you about or been concerned about. Maybe they find it hard to tell you directly, but realize exactly what they were trying to say. Change what you were doing, if you know it's harmful to you, someone else, or anyone's relationship with God. He loves us too much to let us go on by ourselves. Don't be a fool or a mocker. You were made for greater things.

45
Thanks, Grandma!

My grandma died in her ninety-seventh year. What a full life she had! When she told of the old days and how different the times were, I used to love to listen. She talked about seeing her first airplane and automobile and riding her horse to church. Then the horse would go back home all by itself and return at the exact time church was out!

If you've never visited with older people, you have missed a great joy and blessing. Their eyes open so wide with excitement as you approach. They feel so special, as if you were a visiting king or queen. Your touching one arm or hugging older people gives them life, love, and hope. All it takes is a little squeeze of affection.

Grandma spent her last years in a nursing home about a thirty-minute drive from my house. It was never easy to visit her, but I sure felt great while I stayed and as I left. Though I always felt busy, and it was hard to remember to go visit Grandma, my mother felt so good to know that someone had visited her mother that day. Now that she's gone, like so many things, I wish I had the chance to go and be with Grandma for just a little while.

My grandma's favorite saying was, "This too shall pass." Whenever she was in pain she would always say that.

Are you worried about a relationship, schoolwork, or why you feel so bad inside? Grandma never worried much. She always said, "If you can do something about it—do it. If not, forget it!" Remember to say to yourself, *This too shall pass!* Whenever I remember her power phrase, I look up and say, "Thanks, Grandma!"

If you want some wonderful memories and a great feeling inside, visit a nursing home this week with some friends and ask if you can read to someone or run some errands. Read about it from God's Word:

Matthew 25:34–40: "Then the King will say to those on his right, 'Come, you who are blessed by my Father; take your inheritance, the kingdom prepared for you since the creation of the world. For I was hungry and you gave me something to eat, I was thirsty and you gave me something to drink, I was a stranger and you invited me in, I needed clothes and you clothed me, I was sick and you looked after me, I was in prison and you came to visit me.'

"Then the righteous will answer him, 'Lord, when did we see you hungry and feed you, or thirsty and give you something to drink? When did we see you a stranger and invite you in, or needing clothes and clothe you? When did we see you sick or in prison and go to visit you?'

"The King will reply, 'I tell you the truth, whatever you did for one of the least of these brothers of mine, you did for me.'"

The longer you live, the more time you have to realize the value of serving others.

46
Church-Bulletin Humor

Have you ever read your church bulletin, only to find some words rearranged or misplaced, and the end result was a very funny message? Below are some samples from some authentic church bulletins, taken directly from some announcements made in various churches.

This afternoon there will be meetings in the south and north ends of the church. Children will be baptized at both ends.

Tuesday at 4:00 P.M. there will be an ice-cream social. All ladies giving milk, please come early.

Wednesday, the ladies literary society will meet. Mrs. Johnson will sing "Put Me in My Little Bed," accompanied by the pastor.

This being Easter Sunday we will ask Mrs. Brown to come forward and lay an egg on the altar.

The service will close with "Little Drops of Water"; one of the men will start quietly and the rest of the congregation will join in.

The ladies of the church have cast off clothing of every kind, and they can be seen in the church basement on Friday afternoon.

On Sunday a special collection will be taken to defray the expenses of the new carpet. All wishing to do something on the carpet, please come forward and get a piece of paper.

As funny as some of these bulletin mixups are, there is something that happens each week that seems even funnier—but it's not really funny at all. It is the way that we greet one another. We sit next to our neighbor and we act as if he is not there for the rest of the meeting, after we say, "Hello," in the first two minutes. As we walk out of church we try not to bump anyone or make eye contact, and we certainly wouldn't want to introduce ourselves to someone new—it could be embarrassing—or we might not know the exact, perfect word to say.

That is not what God says at all in His Word. He wants us to show people who He is by showing them our love. Please think about this! But don't think too long—you might miss the opportunity to "do" something.

1 John 4:10–12: This is love: not that we loved God, but that he loved us and sent his Son as an atoning sacrifice for our sins. Dear friends, since God so loved us, we also ought to love one another. No one has ever seen God; but if we love each other, God lives in us and his love is made complete in us.

47

It's Just a Job

Think of your friends who have jobs. Think of some of their parents. What attitudes do they possess toward their work? Some might say: "I need it to earn money and that's all," or, "It doesn't bother me to steal from my employer. He makes so much money on me and doesn't pay me very much in the first place," or, "I've got to go to my job, or I'll get fired," or, "Take this job and shove it."

People don't appreciate their employers much these days. A friend of mine owns a supermarket and told me about an employee who was found dealing drugs right in the store, while he was being paid a wage. Of course the employee got fired, of course he had a bad reputation in the area, and he absolutely would not get a good recommendation from my friend. If you are working for someone, is it just a job, or do you appreciate it? Do you come in early and work late? Do you call people by name? Do you learn as much as you can about the industry, business, and customers?

I remember the job I had in a supermarket. My goal was to be the fastest bagger there. Always with a smile, I called people by name and was always happy-go-lucky. As I flipped those cans from one hand to the other and into the sack over and over again, carried the bag out with a smile, opened the door for the people, packed the groceries neatly in the trunk, I would get very nice tips. I soon got moved up to the meat department. Before too long I had my own business. I never took it as a job. I remembered the day my brother had told me, "You are a good worker. Nobody can take that away from you. Don't let them!"

In Bible days many people had an everyday occupation: They were shepherds. Some of those shepherds believed taking care of their sheep was more than just a job. If they had one hundred sheep and one got lost, they went after the one. If the lost one had fallen over a stony cliff in a dangerous spot, a dedicated shepherd would climb down the edge of the mountain and bring that one lost sheep back to safety. He would protect the sheep against wolves and other animals; he would stay up late at night and watch over them. It wasn't just a job for a few hours at a minimum wage, but something he took very seriously and treated it as an important position.

Someone in the Bible is called the Good Shepherd: He treats it as more than just a job, too. Jesus is His name, and watching over His sheep is His game. He loves us and does not want even one of us to stray or fall—to go to hell. Like a shepherd, He cares about us and wants to guide us through the pastures. Jesus wants to bring us to green pastures of living waters; He even said He is the living water. If we drink of Him, we will never again thirst. This means that if we have Christ in our hearts, what we truly need in life is already bought and paid for.

Let Jesus be your shepherd, and remember that on your job your employer believes in you and is paying you a good wage. Give him your best. Give him your all. Let other people say, "I want you to work for me. If that guy doesn't give you a raise, come to me. I will give you one." Watch what happens when you treat your job as your own business—with excitement, enthusiasm, and respect. Be the best you can. *No one can do it for you.*

Besides, in the long run it is not just a job. Colossians 3:23 says, "Whatever you do, work at it with all your heart, as working for the Lord, not for men."

48
Will My Marriage Work?

Many young people today worry so much about getting married, because they see divorce all around them. We have a program entitled "Hope for the Home," for couples, single parents, and young people who are engaged or thinking about marriage. Often young people coming from broken homes fear that they, too, will become divorce statistic material. They wonder, *What should I base my life on? Where did my parents go wrong? Should I attempt a trial marriage?*

All we have to do is look to the first marriage counselor of all time—the most successful one, I might add. What counselor gives totally free advice that is never wrong? This one! He performed the first marriage, because He created the first couple. If we look at what He says about marriage and some guidelines to make it happen in the right way and to keep it going, I don't think you'll have any trouble. That is, of course, if you believe and act on this counselor's advice.

God starts out by saying we need a helpmate.

Genesis 2:18: The Lord God said, "It is not good for the man to be alone. I will make a helper suitable for him."

Genesis 2:24: "For this reason a man will leave his father and mother and be united to his wife, and they will become one flesh."

We should act as one.

Read Ephesians 5:21–33. You will see clearly that God has spelled out how husbands and wives should treat each other, the importance that each should play in the heart and life of his or her mate.

Ephesians 5:31, 32: "For this reason a man will leave his father and mother and be united to his wife, and the two will become one flesh." This is a profound mystery—but I am talking about Christ and the church.

Romans 13:10: Love does no harm to its neighbor. Therefore love is the fulfillment of the law.

Psalms 101:2: I will be careful to lead a blameless life—when will you come to me? I will walk in my house with blameless heart.

Do you think more marriages would be fulfilled if husbands and wives merely followed Proverbs 3:5, 6? It says, "Trust in the Lord with all your heart and lean not on your own understanding; in all your ways acknowledge him, and he will make your paths straight."

When you think about these verses, look over the marriages close to your life and see if you can find out why some work and some do not. Remember, as we all stand individually before the Lord someday, married people are single people with spouses!

49
The Cookie Champ

Markita Andrews did the impossible: She sold 32,000 boxes of Girl Scout cookies, and she's only thirteen years old. She's even written a book called *How to Sell More Cookies, Condos, Cadillacs, Computers . . . and Everything Else.*

She says to young people, "Everyone is in selling. You sell yourself everyday to your friends and teachers in school." Why is the most popular girl in her class the most popular? Markita understands that it's because she's fun and nice to everyone whether or not they're in her clique. Markita says this girl would make a wonderful salesperson, because she likes people, and they like and trust her back.

She also points out why some girls will never be popular. "They put other people down to build themselves up." Her first point to selling yourself is "how to come across." It's not your looks so much as your smile. It's not your clothes as much as it is if you walk and look full of life.

121

How do you come across when you are with people? Do you make prejudgments or say to yourself, *I'll find the good in them?*

You may never sell cookies, but if you want to be a champion at life, meditate on these verses:

Colossians 3:12–15: Therefore, as God's chosen people, holy and dearly loved, clothe yourselves with compassion, kindness, humility, gentleness and patience. Bear with each other and forgive whatever grievances you may have against one another. Forgive as the Lord forgave you. And over all these virtues put on love, which binds them all together in perfect unity.

Let the peace of Christ rule in your hearts, since as members of one body you were called to peace. And be thankful.

Fill your "insides" with God's love, so your "outsides" can share it.

50
The Three Rs in Acting on God's Word

How many times have you heard a good sermon, read a good book, or learned a good lesson and never acted on it?

We all do it every day. Though we set new goals and New Year's resolutions each year, to try to do more of what we know, we often forget them soon. But it need not be that way. Three Rs—*receive, relieve* and *rejoice*—and a little story about my daughter might motivate you to put to work something you have heard in the past.

Receive: While attending a seminar, I learned about different personality temperaments. I learned that my personality was completely different from my little girl Emily's. I am a sanguine (outgoing, always talking, happy, and optimistic), while she is strong willed, moody, and very shy at times. The night before, at a restaurant, when she didn't respond to a friend's good-bye, Holly and I both jumped on her verbally. We said, "If you can't say good-bye to people, when they are talking to you, we won't take you anywhere again. You will have to stay home with a baby-sitter for the rest of your life!" In so many words, we told her that if she didn't respond exactly as we did, we didn't love her and felt ashamed of her.

Relieve: After arriving home from the seminar, I ran in and told Emily, "Guess what Daddy learned today!"

With excitement in her eyes, she said, "What, Daddy?"

"I just found out that you don't have to be like Mommy and Daddy. If you don't feel like saying hello or good-bye, you don't have to. If you want to be quiet and not talk, it's okay, because we love you just the way you are."

She looked as if I had just lifted a million pounds from her little four-year-old frame. With a smile that went from ear to ear and eyes as large as silver dollars, she said, "Oh, thank you, Daddy. I love you so much!"

If you receive a truth and apply it, you will usually relieve a tension or problem. I used the truth I had just learned to relieve a great deal of pressure from my precious little Emily.

Rejoice: Six days later, as Holly, Emily, and I left church, Emily looked up at me and said, "Guess what, Dad? I really love Sunday school and nursery school, and I'm gonna talk more to people from now on." I hugged her and told her how happy I was for her. We rejoiced over her newfound love for being left alone at church and nursery school, because until that day she had clung to us each and every time we took her to either place. On the drive home Holly and I realized how quickly her new attitude came after I relieved her from the burden of having to be as talkative as her professional-speaker dad.

So remember: Use what you receive, and you will usually relieve a pressure or burden, because of the action you have just taken. Then you will have reason for rejoicing, because very few people ever take the time to learn great truths, let alone put them to use.

James very clearly talks about using what we know in God's Word. Put the truths of the Bible into action in your life.

James 1:22: Do not merely listen to the word and so deceive yourselves. Do what it says.

James 2:17: . . . faith by itself, if it is not accompanied by action, is dead.

James 4:17: Anyone, then, who knows the good he ought to do and doesn't do it, sins.

51

Money . . . Money . . . Money!

Dear Bill: It seems our family never has enough money to do anything. No matter how hard my dad looks, he gets jobs for a short while and then loses them. Why is money so important? I sometimes feel that if we could just win the lottery, all of our troubles would be over.

Money . . . money . . . money! Many people feel that if they only had it, their problems would be over. When you face financial trouble, remember that whatever we focus our minds on, they concentrate and dwell on. Often that gets us in deeper and deeper trouble—especially if we think, *I wish I had your money, Why aren't we as well off as those people? Why can't I wear the kind of clothes you wear? If I could only go to your fancy places or had a nice big house, car, boat or lake, like you!* It's not true however, that money will solve every problem. I know people who have it and those who don't. It's what is in the heart that counts, that gives us peace and comfort. God's Word talks a lot about what we can do in financial trouble. Maybe some of His Words will help you now:

Psalms 23:1 (KJV):   The Lord is my shepherd; I shall not want.

Psalms 34:10:   The lions may grow weak and hungry, but those who seek the Lord lack no good thing.

Psalms 37:25:   I was young and now I am old, yet I have never seen the righteous forsaken or their children begging bread.

3 John 2:   Dear friend, I pray that you may enjoy good health and that all may go well with you, even as your soul is getting along well.

Deuteronomy 28:2–8:   All these blessings will come upon you and accompany you if you obey the Lord your God: "You will be blessed in the city and blessed in the country. The fruit of your womb will be blessed, and the crops of your land and the young of your livestock—the calves of your herds and the lambs of your flocks. Your basket and your kneading trough will be blessed. You will be blessed when you come in and blessed when you go out." The Lord will grant that the enemies who rise up against you will be defeated before you. They will come at you from one direction but flee from you in seven. The Lord will send a blessing on your barns and on everything you put your hand to. The Lord your God will bless you in the land he is giving you.

1 Corinthians 16:2:   On the first day of every week, each one of you should set aside a sum of money in keeping with his income, saving it up, so that when I come no collections will have to be made.

Luke 6:38:   "Give, and it will be given to you. A good measure, pressed down, shaken together and running over, will be poured into your lap. For with the measure you use, it will be measured to you."

Many of these verses are really principles to follow. Concentrate on them. Take your mind off of your financial troubles. Instead of saying "More money . . . more money . . . more money," try, "More of God . . . more of God . . .

more of God." If we desire to truly seek Him, His Word says we will find Him and be more contented than the man with a thousand rubies and the cattle on a thousand hills. Loving God is more fun than a jigsaw puzzle with an exciting finish. Stick to it. Keep looking for the treasure of your soul, because God makes one thing very clear in His Word: If you keep looking, you will find it. Then you will be the richest person in the entire world.

52
The Company You Keep

When I grew up, I remember my grandma saying, "Watch the company you keep. Tell me the company you keep, and I'll tell you who you are." Companions are very special persons. Though we are supposed to like everybody, to love everybody, and try to get along with everybody, our companions and friends are special. They influence us for good or bad. I can walk through the mall and go by all kinds of people whom I don't know. Maybe I pass hundreds of people, and none of them influence me to be good, bad, or indifferent. But my friends influence me a great deal by the way they talk, whether or not they steal, if they cheat on tests or not, if they swear, if they drive fast and don't use their seat belts and so on. Because I spend time with my friends, I identify with them. Whether or not I like it, I become part of them.

I strongly challenge you to get help for a friend who has a drinking or drug problem. You will fall into that same problem if you hang around with that person long enough. If a friend of yours steals things, don't let it go along unchecked. If you've got a friend who has a deep inside hurt from a childhood pain, help him talk it out with a counselor or someone who can help him work through it. If you've got a friend who doesn't know the joy of having the creator of the universe living in her heart, help her find God's Son!

"I am a friend to all who fear you, to all who follow your precepts." In that psalm (119:63) David described himself as a companion (a friend) of all those who feared the Lord; he liked people who feared God. By the way, *fear* means "respect and honor." To believe, love, respect, and honor someone means you fear him. It means that you believe he will keep his word. Don't think of fearing God as a negative. When you fear Him, you love, respect, and honor Him.

Do all your friends fear the Lord? Which ones are you so impressed with, while you are with them, that you work very hard to make sure you can go out together, have fun together, and party hearty with? Do they fear God? Do they love Him? Do they respect Him? Do they honor Him? If not, you are keeping the wrong company. You certainly wouldn't want to work for a company where, as soon as you put its name on your résumé, no one else would want to hire you. It is the same with friends. They help you develop your life and act out what you really believe and harbor in your heart. Choose your friends wisely. Make sure you are in good company!

53
Staring at the Sunset

Recently, when Dr. Earl Murphy spoke at our church, he told of a time when at the last minute a church asked him to give a sermon. He didn't have a lot of time to prepare, but he got up and did his best. All through the sermon he noticed people stared right at him—he had their full attention. He could hardly believe it and felt so good about what he had done and how well it had turned out, despite his lack of preparation.

The next evening in this week-long series of meetings, Dr. Murphy sat in the congregation and heard another speaker. As the man began the sermon, Dr. Murphy noticed a beautiful sight directly behind the speaker's head. This church had a large window, and a mountain range lay just behind it, with the mountaintops covered with snow. The window acted as a frame for a beautiful picture of God's handiwork. Five minutes into the sermon, the sun began to set. All through the sermon, for about thirty-five minutes, the sun fell lower and lower. Reds turned into oranges and all different shades of crimson that only God could paint.

Then and there Dr. Murphy realized that he hadn't been

such a great speaker after all. People didn't stare and sit on the edges of their seats because of what he preached, but because they watched what God was doing. He had to chuckle, for this illustrated a beautiful lesson for all of us—especially whenever we do something great for God.

When we serve Him, do we want people to look at us or to notice what God is doing? As I share with young people one-on-one after my meetings, I think about this. Because I have the Creator of the universe living in my heart, and He strengthens me and gives me the wisdom, I feel I can handle life and anything it throws at me.

Sometimes I want people to notice me. Every now and then, when I give a talk, things run smoothly, and I am in control, as if I have the audience in the palm of my hand, and I think, *I'm really something.* Then and there God zaps me with forgetting the next line, remembering that my marriage would not be together, if it weren't for Him, or realizing that I wouldn't have this calling if God did not give me the gift. He reminds me how he caused a publishing company to call and ask me to write a book. This is the truth, my friend. There is very little room for pride when you think about the hurt you have caused God and all of the wonderful things He's done for you.

Notice the beauty around you that only God can paint. It might be a sunset, but it also might be some wild flowers along the side of the road, the laughter of a four-year-old, the innocent question of your younger brother, asking you if he could be your friend, or maybe even something greater. The next time you do something for God, are you doing it so people can watch, notice, and feel His majesty—His mightiness—His forgiveness—His love; or are you doing it so they will think you are great? All of us need to look at these questions every day.

My friend Gary Thompson challenged me to memorize Romans 8:32. I believe it will help you notice what God is doing in your life and in the lives of others: "He who did not spare his own Son, but gave him up for us all—how will he not also, along with him, graciously give us all things?"

God says here that He did not spare Jesus, His only Son, but gave Him to us. Since He has done that, won't He gladly and graciously give us all things? Next to Jesus, everything is inferior. God has already given us the greatest gift—His *only* Son. He wants you to know that if you live for Him, He will give you every joy your heart will ever know or long for. Notice what God is doing. Look at His beauty today. God bless you!

54

It Starts With C

"What is the number-one thing that causes a person— especially a teenager—to feel inferior?" Can you think of something, more than anything else, that causes us to experience low self-esteem and feel worthless? Most people —teenagers and parents alike—get it wrong. When I ask this question, I get every possible answer. I hear: "Fear," "Family situation," "IQ," "Abilities," "Looks," "Wealth," "Low self-esteem," "Other people," "Peer pressure," "Drugs," and so on, but rarely do I hear the right answer.

Then I share, "It starts with C." I hear words like: *communication, compliance, not caring, lack creativity,* but they still don't get it.

Have you gotten it yet? Think of yourself in school, feeling inferior. Think of whom in you feel inferior to, and you will have the key to knowing how we become and feel inferior. Around certain people you feel inferior, and around others you do not.

Realize that you have a sure-fire way of never feeling inferior to anyone, anywhere, at anytime. It will help you feel great about yourself at all times. However, most people don't know anything about this marvelous secret. They go through life, and if someone does something that affects them, they make statements like: "He made me feel this way," or, "She knew I would feel this way because of what she did." No one *makes* you do anything. You *choose* to do it. The elevator does not make people scared. Have you ever heard of an elevator sneaking up behind someone and yelling *boo?* Heights do not make people frightened. Airplanes don't yell "I'm gonna get you!" at people when they fly. We choose to be frightened in these situations.

The thing that makes people feel inferior is *comparison.* When you compare yourself to others, you will always fall short, because in any skill, talent, subject, or sport, other people will always do it better than you do. Someone can run faster than you, will get better grades than you, and so on. Comparison is deadly and destructive.

I play on a basketball team with eight or nine of the greatest guys in the world. We have been together now for four or five years. It means so much to me to be with them that I have actually flown home from engagements on more expensive flights, so I could be at the game or the practice. At times I watch someone score twelve, fifteen or twenty points, and I keep saying, *How come I only score two or four points?* I think that my game high in five years has been six points. I watch the guys run with the greatest of ease, and they can jump. (I did get off the ground three inches one time. My wife told me I was exaggerating, but it felt as if I was up there.) I keep comparing and wishing I could do that, but then I realize that they have been gifted with the ability to run faster and jump higher. Besides, most of them have played for a long time, but I never played in high school. It took me two years just to get a sense of the court and to know where I was supposed to be at the right time. Once a team member grabbed the ball on the rebound, and I stood there blocking him as everyone else ran down the court. He said to me, "I'm on your side. Turn around. Let's go the other way." We both had a good laugh.

Think about this: If you were the only person in your school, you might feel lonely, but you would not feel inferior. You don't need to stay all alone in order to have a new attitude. You just have to put comparison in the right perspective.

God's Word makes it very clear to whom and how we are to make comparisons:

2 Corinthians 10:12, 13:   We do not dare to classify or compare ourselves with some who commend themselves. When they measure themselves by themselves and compare themselves with themselves, they are not wise. We, however, will not boast beyond proper limits, but will confine our boasting to the field God has assigned to us, a field that reaches even to you.

55
The Unpardonable Sin

"Dear Bill: I think I have committed the unpardonable sin. What can I do?"

When I get letters like this one, I realize that many people don't know what the unpardonable sin is. You would know if you had committed it, because your heart would be so hardened that no spiritual impression would ever again come to your soul. If you had committed it, you wouldn't even write to me, concerned about the unpardonable sin.

Matthew 12:31, 32:   "And so I tell you, every sin and blasphemy will be forgiven men, but the blasphemy against the Spirit will not be forgiven. Anyone who speaks a word against the Son of Man will be forgiven, but anyone who speaks against the Holy Spirit will not be forgiven, either in this age or in the age to come."

Mark 3:28, 29:   "I tell you the truth, all the sins and blasphemies of men will be forgiven them. But whoever blasphemes against the Holy Spirit will never be forgiven; he is guilty of an eternal sin."

Both passages above tell us that speaking against the Holy Spirit and blaspheming against Him never has forgiveness. Since the Holy Spirit is God's agent now that Jesus has risen, to blaspheme against Him means that when God tugs on your heart to accept Christ as your personal Savior, and you repeatedly say no over and over again, you have committed the unpardonable sin. To blaspheme the Holy Spirit literally means to spit in His face, talk against Him when He is calling you and touching your heart to accept Christ as your Savior.

Realize that murder is not unpardonable; David confessed his sin and was forgiven. (Look that up in Psalms 32:5.) Theft is not unpardonable. The penitent thief on the cross was pardoned (see Luke 23:43). Blaspheming in and of itself is not unpardonable. Paul was pardoned for this very thing (read 1 Timothy 1:13). Adultery is not unpardonable; the woman of Samaria was saved (John 4:28, 29).

God will forgive your sins; He wants to make you whole. Don't worry about the unpardonable sin. Instead accept Christ as your Savior, ask forgiveness for your sins, and recognize what Christ did on the cross—He paid the entire price.

Isaiah 55:7: Let the wicked forsake his way and the evil man his thoughts. Let him turn to the Lord, and he will have mercy on him, and to our God, for he will freely pardon.

God wants you to return to Him, no matter what state you are in. He will abundantly pardon. Grow in your faith. Don't let Satan, the great deceiver, keep you in bondage any longer.

56

One of Those Magic Moments

My mother was in the hospital about to have what we thought was a fairly routine operation on her throat. Though we all prayed very hard for her recovery and the success of the surgery, none of us realized the severity of the operation until we met with the doctor the night before. He told us it was a very delicate situation because my mother could come out of this operation never speaking again.

That evening before nurses took her to be prepped for the morning operation, a lot of tension and anxiety filled the hospital room. We all tried to remain cheerful, but I'm sure our concern showed through a little bit. My mother was as strong as I've ever seen her. I've never been prouder of her—or my younger brother Dale. Dale interrupted the conversation, "Mother, I would like to have you listen to something." He turned on the radio, and at that precise moment the D.J. was set up on the local radio station to say, "Mrs. Sanders, this is for you, from your family. We want you to know that we are all praying for you, and we also want you to know that God has got it all in control." At that moment he cued up and played B. J. Thomas's song "He's Got It All in Control."

As we sat there the tears flowed, and we all relaxed in God's presence and into the comfort of knowing that no matter what situation we face in life (even a chance of never speaking again or seeing your mother scared and your father just as scared for her), God indeed has us in the palm of his hand. He cares for us more than we will ever know or imagine. He loves us so much that He sent His Son to die for us. No matter what each of us face today, just like that moment in my family's past, He's got it all in control.

Why don't we give God the controls? He's waiting. I know as I look back at that evening in the hospital room, it was a magical moment for all of us, because God was there. One of my goals for this year is to make more magic moments in my family. Instead of just looking back and saying, "Those were the days," I want these to be the days. I want these to be the days for you, too. What can you do for another family member today to let him know that God has it in control, to let her know that you care enough to go to the radio station to get this all taken care of ahead of time and work out all the details. Do something for your brother, sister, mom, or dad. I know you can. Make a magic moment today. It will even be more special if you let someone know that God's got it all in control. He's waiting to take control—just give it to Him.

Revelation 3:20:   "Here I am! I stand at the door and knock. If anyone hears my voice and opens the door, I will come in and eat with him, and he with me."

Let Jesus enter your heart and look what He brings with Him. Romans 5:1 (TLB, italics added) says: "So now, since we have been made right in God's sight by faith in his promises, *we can have real peace* with him because of what Jesus Christ our Lord has done for us."

57
Hurts on the Inside

Dear Bill: When I grew up I was sexually abused by my brother. It lasted for several years, and no one knew anything about it. That's a long time ago, and I am a Christian now, but I still feel much pain and guilt inside. Please help! Your friend, Hurting.

Dear Hurting: I am so sorry that you had to experience such an ongoing nightmare. Child abuse and abuse of any kind, whether sexual, physical, mental, or emotional, leave scars that last for a long time. There are some helpful steps that I would like to share with you:

1. You need to realize that it was *not* your fault. You were the victim.
2. Bathe yourself in God's Word and His love. Read the Bible. Find out just how much God loves you. Read accounts of how Jesus died on the cross, was beaten and spat upon, and how He must have hurt, as well.
3. Confess any known sin and accept God's forgiveness. Realize that He has certainly forgiven you for any part you think you might have played, especially since you were just the victim. Whether or not you caused it to happen,

God's forgiveness is complete. Read 1 John 1:9 and realize that He forgives all our confessed sins.

4. Forgive your brother (Matthew 6:14). Many times people harbor guilt, pain, shame, and hurt from the past because anger won't let it escape. If that is the case with you, go to a quiet place, turn it over to God, and truly tell God you forgive your brother. I might add that most likely your brother has also been hurting deeply all these years. He doesn't want to bring it up, and he is afraid to see you or talk about it. Many times brothers and sisters with situations like this never see each other for years and years; if they get together for Christmas, they sit quietly and never go in the same room or talk. The pain just lingers.

5. Try to go to your brother and tell him you forgive him. You don't need to mention any details; he will know what you are talking about. Just say, "When we were growing up, many of the things that happened . . . well, I have forgiven you for all of them." This will make you the bigger person and really put you in harmony with God's way of restoring relationships, feelings, and self-dignity (Matthew 5:41).

6. Talk it out! Seek a good biblical counselor. Find a counselor who believes that the final authority of everything we deal with must be God's Word. Bring your pain, hurt, and anger out in the open. Many times your counselor will want you to share what actually happened so you can get it out and deal with it. Check out your counselor very closely before meeting, but once you find one whom you can trust, make sure you go for at least four or five sessions. If your pain still lingers, there are group sessions where you can share with people, to hear about their victories.

7. Ask for forgiveness from anyone you have hurt. Quite often sin leads to more sin. People who are abused sometimes abuse others, get involved with premarital sex, or have affairs outside marriage. Whatever it may have been, seek God's forgiveness. If your sin did not take place too long

ago, go to the person and seek forgiveness as well. If that person is married and has a family, then drop it. If you dated years ago and can't locate someone, then forget it. Don't let anyone tell you that because you didn't meet with a person, the sin remains and forgiveness will not take place. God does not want you to startle an entire family or to break a relationship between that person, a spouse, or family members. God wants you to come to Him and let Him cleanse you.

As you read this, maybe you're thinking, *I've never been abused sexually.* But someone near you (either in your family, your class, your school, or where you work) probably has been treated unfairly in the past, abused, and harbors much guilt. Loan this book to that person so he or she can read the steps that will bring a peaceful life. I would also encourage you to help that person focus on the fact that Jesus knows what it is to hurt, feel pain, and have anger, fear, and frustration.

When Jesus was in the Garden of Gethsemane, He was afraid. He knew that in a little while God the Father would totally abandon Him. He would have to enter hell itself in order to take our place there. He didn't concentrate on rising from the dead, but He hurt because He saw what lay right in front of Him. Notice what He did to eliminate his fears and inner hurt: He chose to do God's will. The steps I have given you are not easy and not popular, but they are God's way.

God's way—forgiveness, moving forward, forgetting, and getting help—is not what the world has taught us to do, feel, and act on in situations like these. The world would have us be angry and get even. Like David, in the Old Testament, do you have a Goliath (a giant) in your life? With God's help and your hand on the slingshot, you, too, can kill that emotional monster in your life. (Read 1 Samuel 17.)

1 Samuel 17:49: Reaching into his bag and taking out a stone, he slung it and struck the Philistine on the forehead. The stone sank into his forehead, and he fell facedown on the ground.

58
Are You Planning to Fail?

Just a while ago I heard a catchy, powerful statement: "If you fail to plan, you plan to fail."

Do we have plans in front of us? What kind of blueprints do we follow for our lives? An engineer builds a skyscraper by continually checking the blueprints—the plans. As the work begins and the hole is prepared, when he wants to start the cement work for the foundation, he looks over the blueprint to make sure he's on target.

What do our life plans look like? Do they follow the plans of the world, or God's plan? Do we just go along and do whatever we want whenever we feel like it—with whatever crowd or in whatever activity happens to be in front of us?

A builder starts from the bottom up; the foundation is the first part of any powerful structure. If it isn't sturdy, the building will fall. Likewise those who build their lives on the wrong foundation will also fall. Of course, marriages that fail to plan end up failing—it's called divorce. The foundation for many marriages is do whatever you want whenever you want, don't plan ahead financially, spiritually, communicationwise, or emotionally. Such structures fall into the water (like a building founded on a sandy beach), and the people drown.

When do we need a firm foundation? When do we need to plan ahead, and what do we need to plan ahead for? We certainly don't need to plan for the good days, when we sail on calm waters and the problems have disappeared. No, we need to plan ahead for the times when life is tough.

Matthew 7:26: "But everyone who hears these words of mine and does not put them into practice is like a foolish man who built his house on sand."

Luke 6:46–49: "Why do you call me, 'Lord, Lord,' and do not do what I say? I will show you what he is like who comes to me and hears my words and puts them into practice. He is like a man building a house, who dug down deep and laid the foundation on rock. When a flood came, the torrent struck that house but could not shake it, because it was well built. But the one who hears my words and does not put them into practice is like a man who built a house on the ground without a foundation. The moment the torrent struck that house, it collapsed and its destruction was complete."

We need solid rock under our feet when the earth and everyone around us seems to be unstable:

1 Corinthians 3:10–15: By the grace God has given me, I laid a foundation as an expert builder, and someone else is building on it. But each one should be careful how he builds. For no one can lay any foundation other than the one already laid, which is Jesus Christ. If any man builds on this foundation using gold, silver, costly stones, wood, hay or straw, his work will be shown for what it is, because the Day will bring it to light. It will be revealed with fire, and the fire will test the quality of each man's work. If what he has built survives, he will receive his reward. If it is burned up, he will suffer loss; he himself will be saved, but only as one escaping through the flames.

Jesus is the only secure foundation for any of us. I like 1 Corinthians 3:11, especially, "For no one can lay any foundation other than the one already laid, which is Jesus Christ." If you are a child of God, His Word (the Bible) is your blueprint—plan. Don't go through life without it!

59
Practice Makes____?

Fill in the blank: Practice makes _____! You said *perfect*, right? Wrong. Practice does not make perfect. To prove it, have you ever golfed? Jack Nicklaus has been practicing golf much more than most of us, and he doesn't get a hole in one even 1 percent of the time.

Reggie Smith taught me that practice makes permanent patterns of performance. Whatever you practice becomes a permanent pattern or habit. Practice tying your shoes when you are little, and you won't even have to think of it now—you just do it. The same with daily Bible reading, saying, "I love you," to your parents, or fighting with your brothers and sisters. Good study habits, feeling good about yourself, saying no and yes at the right times are all things we can practice in order to make them automatic.

Being perfect is only attainable when we enter Jesus' presence in heaven. Earthly perfectionists often have the toughest time enjoying life, because they expect too much from themselves, their families, and their friends. If your mother is a perfectionist and expects your room to be spotless and your grades to be perfect, give her this free tip that will help her enjoy life a little more: "Let the house go for a few months. Go to the grocery store and only buy junk food. Have a pillow fight with your kids."

Be easy on yourself. God doesn't demand that you be the smartest, the fastest, the prettiest (thank goodness), the best dressed, or the most popular. He only wants your love and faith. Read Matthew 22:36–40. Make these two greatest commandments permanent patterns of performance, and you'll have God's thumbs up!

60
The Wrong Kind of Laughter

Several years ago I went to the library with a prayer in my heart. I wanted to come up with a poem that would depict all the different ways and different types of people whom we put down in school. As I sat there, God gave me each and every one of these verses within about an hour and a half. I have never studied this, but had it instantly memorized. I present it in each and every student assembly I give.

It's wrong to put down—
The new student, the poor student,
the one who walks funny and talks funny.
Let's call him skinny and call her fat,
and, "What kind of shirt do you even call that?"
"Hey, giraffe, how'd you get so tall?"
and, "You're so short you've got no place to fall."
Check out buckteeth, and look at those ears,
"Hey, elephant nose, why all the tears?"

And the one with no friends, she eats all alone,
bet we could make her cry all the way home.
Let's laugh at that guy, he got cut from the team,
"You're the worst player we've ever seen!"
And she was too chicken to stay with the play,
"It's cause she talks funny and forgot what to say."

I heard his parents both left home,
"If you weren't adopted, you'd be all alone."
Hey, her mother's real sick, oh, that's too bad,
"Don't wait around for us to be sad."

Look who's coming, it's crater face,
I'm glad I don't have zits all over the place,
"You're just a loser, you'll never win,"
and, "How dare you come to our school,
with the wrong color skin?"

Yes, we're the populars, we have to be cool,
and as you've seen, we can sure be cruel.
But as long as you do all the things that we say,
you, too, can be privileged with our group to play,

but there's no security being part of our team,
we even turn on our own, as you've probably seen.
But if you're cute and handsome and really smart,
why you'll fit in right from the start.

But you must never disagree,
And for heaven's sake, don't turn ugly,
or we'll kick you out, right into the street,
for us to be popular, we'd even cheat.

We don't believe in the things from above,
like honesty, integrity, and brotherly love.
Society's taught us to be number one.
Who cares if you're hurt? We're having fun.

It's not just students we pick on each day,
but anyone who's different and gets in our way.
Society has taught us, don't worry what you say,
and forget the consequences past today.

We also pick on teachers who are old and shy,
and we love to make the bus driver cry.
And the cook, last week we threw food right in his
face,
and the counselors and subs we love to disgrace.

And of course the principal we always boo;
it's nothing personal, just the thing to do.
And there's Mom, whom we're mad at, and Dad, who's
unfair,
of all the nerve, yesterday he even asked me to move a
chair.

I've covered them all, so I'm ready to stop. . . .
But wait, there's one more, I almost forgot,
It's my dear, charming brother, who puts chips in my
pop. . . .

Please help me wipe out the wrong kind of laughter in your school, where you work, and in your town. Together, we can keep sadness and pain only on the six o'clock news and not in our own backyards. In Matthew 25:40 Jesus taught us much more clearly about the wrong kind of laughter: "'. . . I tell you the truth, whatever you did for one of the least of these brothers of mine, you did for me.'"

61
The Man From Pinch

Have you ever been in a pinch and ne_ded a friend to rescue you? I have, and one day I was rescued by "the man from Pinch." His name is E. Larry Moles, and he comes from Lima, Ohio. By those of us in the speaking profession, he is known across the country as one of the most caring, gentle, sharing, loving, and kind big men you have ever seen in your life. He is a hugger. He tells people that you need ten to twenty hugs just to make it, and even more to grow on. He will hug you in an airport, in a plane, in a restaurant—it doesn't matter. He hands out roses to his audiences, and he tells them "I love you." This giant of a man, with an even bigger heart, taught me so many things.

One morning I had a rea problem. I live in Michigan, and I had a talk in mid-Ohio. A friend of mine planned to fly me there in his private plane, but the night before, fog set in, and my friend called me bright and early the next morning to say, "I can't fly you there this morning for your 9:00 A.M. talk. It is too foggy, and they won't let me leave the airport. I feel so bad, but there is nothing I can do about it."

"That's okay," I answered. "We'll find a way." As I hung up the phone, I started thinking. *Who, from my great bunch of friends from the National Speaker's Association, can I call to take over for me?* Boom—it hit me like lightning—Larry Moles, the man from Pinch. I called Larry at about 5:30 A.M. When he answered, I asked if he knew where the little town I'd planned to speak in was. He had no idea. I told him what I knew, and he said, "Don't worry about it. Give me the man's name and phone number, and I'll be on my way. I'll call you back in twenty minutes." Twenty minutes later he had showered and called me back, and I gave him the details. On one of his few days off, he drove from his home, got lost several times, but made it into the auditorium with five hundred kids waiting, and he gave a tremendous speech. He challenged them to be all they can be, to love and not hate, to learn wherever possible, never to destroy— but only build up people and life.

When I talked to Larry later, I told him that I was only getting paid a little bit for the speech, because I was newer in the business than he was. I offered to make up the difference between my fee and his. He said, "No way. I will do it for that fee and no more. You were in need, and I came to your rescue—that is all there is to it."

When you are in a pinch, it is nice to have a friend who sticks tight like glue. Surround yourself with at least two or three people whom you can call on when you get in a jam.

If you are a Christian, you already have one Friend like that. No matter what jams we get ourselves into, the Lord is always there. God gave me the presence of mind and peace of heart not to get angry at my friend who didn't know how to fly in the fog, not to get angry at the world, get upset and go berserk. If I hadn't been calm that day, I would not have been able to present myself clearly at 5:30 in the morning, and maybe Larry would not have come to my aid after all.

Whenever you get in a jam, God is there waiting to help. Sometimes He will be there in the form of an idea; He gave me the thought of calling Larry. Had I gotten all nervous, I could have called up the school and just said that I couldn't make it. As it was, the kids were winners, Larry was a winner. I was a winner—and everything worked out great!

Make a list of two or three friends whom you could call if you absolutely had to, under any circumstance. I think in all of our lives there is a friend from Pinch—we just need to look around and identify him ahead of time. Cement that relationship and make it grow. Never take your friend for granted. Always put in and never take out, and watch what happens. Your friend will be there when you need him. Whenever you are in a jam like that, pray and ask, "Who is my man from Pinch?"

Philippians 4:4–7: Rejoice in the Lord always. I will say it again: Rejoice! Let your gentleness be evident to all. The Lord is near. Do not be anxious about anything, but in everything, by prayer and petition, with thanksgiving, present your requests to God. And the peace of God, which transcends all understanding, will guard your hearts and your minds in Christ Jesus.

62
Never Too Late to Try

I'm a great believer in seat belts. Once I saw a movie entitled *There's Room to Live*, which pointed out that between your nose and the windshield, there's room to live. However, once you start smashing your head into the windshield at sixty miles an hour, the room and the opportunities for life greatly diminish. In this documentary several policemen said they have never pulled a dead person in a seat belt out of a car. I am sure it has happened before, but they had not done it, nor had they heard of any policeman doing it.

What happens whenever we talk about seat belts? Someone nearby always says she doesn't use them and gives you a reason or two—and she tries to sell you on the idea that *you* shouldn't use seat belts either. The greatest excuse I have ever heard from a young person came from a teen who told me, "I don't wear them because I don't like anything touching my body." (We all know that's a lie.) Another fellow told me that he doesn't wear seat belts because he heard about a guy who was in a wreck, flew out of the car, landed in a bale of hay, and without the dive he would have died. Then the classic, "I don't wear them because I don't want to get caught in a wreck or a fire and not be able to get out." I tell these people that if they don't have enough strength at that moment to push the seat belt button, they are not going to have enough strength to open the door.

If you've never worn a seat belt before, then it is never too late to try. Some time ago I spoke to several hundred teachers in one school system, and along with my material helping teachers to be "life touchers," touching students' lives, along with teaching the subject, I challenged each one to wear his or her seat belt. A year later, when I returned to the school, the superintendent met me and said, "There's a woman here whom you must meet." He said, "Actually you met her when you were here last year, but you've got to hear her story." This delightful teacher shared with me that after my talk she had not worn her seat belt, but it kind of haunted her and bugged her for several months. One day, about five months after I visited her school, she was driving down the road and felt inspired to pull over and put on her seat belt. Moments later she was hit by a train, and without her seat belt she would have been killed.

I don't care if it is seat belts or doing what you know you should do in a certain area of your life. Remember, *it's never too late to start*. Start today. One of the oldest and most trite statements you have ever heard or will ever hear says, "Today is the first day of the rest of your life." But guess what? *It is true*. It is never too late to start, too late to try, too late to do what you know you should do, could do, can do, and will do. Don't let old man procrastination talk you into another moment's delay before you get down to business with your potential and the opportunities at hand. Look at your future, set those goals, dig back in your mind, and find out what you have been told over and over about your potential or the opportunities at hand. Remember that it's never too late to try—and get on with it. The world needs you. Great things are going to happen to you, and you've got to be there when they do. You've got to be prepared, or they will pass you by.

For safety's sake, for the love of your family and friends, and for the future awaiting you, *buckle up!* In most states it is the law, but wear your seat belt if you love any member of your family. The reason is simple, if you get in a car accident and end up in a coma, killed, or maimed, you do your family no good. The hurt and pain you cause isn't worth a few moments of not putting on your seat belt.

God always asks us to bear and share the burdens. Catch the life-giving balance in these verses showing the laws of love and responsibility:

Galatians 6:2, 5:   Carry each other's burdens, and in this way you will fulfill the law of Christ [love]. . . . For each one should carry his own load [responsibility].

63

"It Is to Me!"

I had been in a school all day, doing five different assemblies on self-esteem, peer pressure, the power of laughter and saying no to things that hurt you. As I talk and share during my talks I also look! I usually see the same things: hurting kids, masks too thick to take off, the cool kids and the easy-to-pick-on kids. There's always one common denominator: young people hungry for help. After the talk they line up for counseling. They are supposed to go to class, but they don't care. They trust me, and they are desperate for hope! A suggestion, a listening ear, some advice, *anything!*

The last one in line was sixteen and very attractive, but she looked as if she carried the entire student body on her back. "I have nothing to live for. I want to die. Can you help?" I listened and held her as she shared her problem. Her boyfriend of two years had just broken up with her!

I couldn't believe it. I thought, *There are thousands of boys. Boys and girls are breaking up every day. Meanwhile people are starving to death and homeless all over the world.* So in my wisdom of thirty-some years, I said, "That's not the end of the world." With every ounce of energy and anguish she could, she spoke one powerful sentence: *"It is to me!"*

In just four words, she taught me the lesson of a lifetime —one for each of us to remember. When someone hurts, her hurt is all that matters! Until she gets over that particular hurt, nothing else is important. Absolutely nothing!

We found that teen help. When you need help and things get hard to handle, use these three steps that I shared with her:

Step 1: *Put things into perspective.* I asked her how she would feel if she were telling me this same story, only one thing was different: She was blind. She admitted in that situation her boyfriend would take on much less importance. Read 1 Chronicles 16:30; thank the Lord today for all the wonderful things He has given you, and your problems won't be out of focus!

Step 2: *Replace your worry with prayer.* "Don't worry about anything, instead, pray about everything; tell God your needs and don't forget to thank him for his answers. If you do this you will experience God's peace, which is far more wonderful than the human mind can understand. His peace will keep your thoughts and your hearts quiet and at rest as you trust

Christ Jesus (Philippians 4:6, 7 TLB.) She started focusing on the key phrases in this verse ("pray," "tell God your needs," "thank him," "God's peace," "wonderful," "keep . . . your hearts quiet," and "trust Christ"), and her depression and pain melted away.

Step 3: *Look forward, not behind.* Think on Philippians 3:13 for a moment before you end this special time with God.

Remember, our problems and concerns are a matter of perspective and focus. What we think about, we act out. Think on the good things Jesus has for you and have a wonderful day! Feed your brain with something sane—read your Bible.

64
Communicate Well

Good communication can help you in school, in your career, and anytime you address an audience or speak with friends. Follow these Ten Commandments of Good Communication to make a big change in your life:

1. *Be accurate.* Violating this rule can really get you into trouble.
2. *Be brief.*
3. *Be clear.* Avoid complex word combinations—phrases

that have double meanings or parts that might be misunderstood.

4. *Don't try to impress your audience.* Speak in terms they can understand.
5. *Consider your audience.* Whenever you write or speak, use language that clearly shows your audience that you know who they are.
6. *Think and organize before you write or speak.*
7. *Make your message interesting.* Say something worthwhile, then dress it up with a little humor, some anecdotes, a story or two, and so on.
8. *Don't leave out essential facts.* Remember the five Ws: *Who, What, When Where,* and *Why*—and *How!*
9. *Be ethical.* Be fair with everyone whom you work with in any type of communication. Always give credit where credit is due. (For instance, I got these commandments from my good friends at Business Professionals of America. Jody VanCooney assembled a booklet entitled "Verbal Communications: File of Ideas.")
10. *Don't just relate it—illustrate it.* Use actual objects, models, movies, photos, and drawings whenever you can.

Even though you may never give a formal speech, address a large audience, or accept an award, you still need to know these tips. Lack of proper communication skills is the number-one cause of divorces and bankruptcies. Family and business failures happen because people do not communicate properly.

If you have the chance to give a talk, remember the greatest communicator of all time: Jesus. Did He just give facts, or did He share the most powerful tool known to mankind—accurate, powerful storytelling? He was accurate, brief, clear, and He talked in terms His audience could understand. Jesus used everyday objects for examples, was always organized, and made His talks very interesting—at times thousands of people followed Him. He invented the word *ethical,* and He sure knew how to illustrate it.

Why not take a look at one of His famous parables and see how it can apply to your life? (Read about the rich fool in Luke 12:16–21.) There is a phrase in there that shows up quite often in today's language. ". . . Take life easy; eat, drink and be merry" (v. 19). Notice what God says immediately after that statement—two words: "You fool!" Jesus is not condemning money itself, but He realizes it is one of the greatest hindrances to spiritual growth—unless it is as dedicated as our life must be. Then it can make an influence in promoting the kingdom of heaven. Remember this powerful statement: "A man's true wealth is that which is still possessed when all that death can take is taken." God has communicated very clearly and accurately. Let's listen to His wise words when we hear them. Filter His Words through your head and place them in your heart.

Luke 12:19, 20: "And I'll say to myself, ' "You have plenty of good things laid up for many years. Take life easy; eat, drink and be merry.' " But God said to him, 'You fool! This very night your life will be demanded from you. Then who will get what you have prepared for yourself?' "

65
Just a Little Time

Both my parents work, so we never spend time together.

Work, meetings, committees, and bowling seem to take up all your time. I wish we could have a special night when we could be together . . . just you and me.

Why can't we go on vacations in the summer, like we used to? I just wish things could be the way they were when I was younger and our family was all together.

Time—they say it is what life is made of. Each of us has the same twenty-four hours every day. We can yell, fuss, borrow, or steal, and we will never get any more or any less. We always hear people say, "There just isn't enough time"; "I wish I had more time to do this"; or "Why does time have to fly by so fast that we never have any time for fun?"

I learned a long time ago, and the three young people who wrote these letters to their parents also know, that in the eyes of a son or daughter, love is a four-letter word spelled t-i-m-e. We always hear speakers talk about quality time versus quantity time, and in my opinion, many parents feel that a few short quality minutes with their son or daughter will replace being together for a much longer and greatly needed period of time. Though quality and quantity time both have their merits, I feel the quantity of time spent together is most important.

What do you do if your parents don't spend enough time with you? Go and share with them that you value your time together. Thank them for the time they *have* spent with you. Remind them of the good times and how those memories mean so very much to you. Then ask if you could have a "date night" with one of your parents. Once a week, just the two of you, to do something special. You might go out to dinner and then bowl or run errands together, or it might mean Saturday-morning shopping. My wife has fond memories of going to the hardware store on Saturday mornings with her dad. On the way home they would stop in the soda shop and get a treat.

I remember my dad coming home from work, and before he even went into the house to have his cup of coffee and read the newspaper, he would set his lunch pail down on the steps and come to the backyard to throw the baseball to me for an hour or two. My mother baby-sat us all the time. We played "hide the thimble" on rainy days, and I remember the great amounts of time she spent encouraging me with my animals. I used to raise everything from pigeons to rabbits.

Spend time with your parents. It is hard for them to understand teenagers and young people growing up. You have your own friends; you'd rather be at the mall than at home; quite often you don't like to tell your parents where you are going, because you feel you have become an adult. They find this all very confusing. It's been a long time since they've been teenagers, and times have certainly changed. Help them understand you. Help them want to spend more time with you.

In digging through God's Word, I found a comforting verse for each of us who feels someone in the family (especially Mom or Dad) has forgotten us for a time or seems too busy with a career, friends, meetings, or whatever. No matter if any of our loved ones forget us, God will not. He will be there for us always.

Isaiah 49:15, 16   "Can a mother forget the baby at her breast and have no compassion on the child she has borne? Though she may forget, I will not forget you! See, I have engraved you on the palms of my hands; your walls are ever before me."

Use the steps I've described to go to your parents and explain your need for their time. In the meantime, go to God's Word and concentrate on His words. He's got all the time in the world.

66

"Stop Picking on Me"

Dear Bill: . . . No one likes me. They always call me names and pick on me. I try to ignore them, but I can't. You don't know the pain I feel. I just want to be accepted. . . .

I get letters like this one almost every week. Each and every time I speak at a high school, several people tell me the pain of being picked on. If you feel like this, follow these steps to help yourself:

1. *Learn to ignore it.* If you give people a payoff (crying; getting mad; running to your teacher, parents, or principal; or merely letting them know you are bothered by their words), they will keep on bugging you. I know it's hard to do, but you *must* ignore it.
2. *Realize they are immature and usually possess low self-esteem.* People like to pull others down to their level, because somehow it makes them feel better. Don't let others use you as a doormat or the butt of their jokes.
3. *Get busy.* Stay active and involved. If you have goals to reach and people to help you, you will walk faster and feel better about yourself. In my book *Tough Turf,* I list twenty-

five steps you can take to enlarge your self-esteem until you feel good enough about yourself to laugh at yourself.

4. *Focus on the people with you.* Luke 9:50 tells us: ". . . Jesus said, 'For whoever is not against you is for you.'" If five teens pick on you, remember that the other three hundred in your school are on your side.

5. *Laugh at yourself.* One teen told me he had a better putdown about himself than anyone else. The others would call him a name, and he would say something twice as bad. (Read Matthew 5:40, 41.)

6. *Love your enemies.* You may win them for Christ. Read Matthew 5:43–48 and see what it has to say. Matthew 5:44 commands: ". . . Love your enemies and pray for those who persecute you."

7. *Get creative.* Look for new ways of making your enemies into friends. Two bullies were calling a little guy in on a fight. The little fellow drew a line on the ground and said to the biggest one, "I dare you to step over that line!" He did. Then the little guy put his arm around the big guy and said, "Good. Now you are on my side!"

8. *Pray for them.* Pray for their very souls. You will then see them as God does: lost, hurting, and alone. When you see them as God does, you'll feel love instead of anger

If you need a friend, you've got one in God and me. Write me and I'll talk to you through the mail. My address is in the back of this book.

67
The Starfish

A good friend of mine, Gary Thompson, has a marvelous program educating teachers, parents, and young people about preventing suicide. Recently he told me the story of a starfish and a little boy. It touched my heart.

A little boy was walking along the seashore with his friend and sharing how the tides threw starfish out of the sea and onto the beach. When the low tide came in, the starfish couldn't move fast enough to get back in the water. Left defenseless on the beach, it would dry up and die. The little boy finally saw a starfish. He picked it up, and just as he was getting ready to throw it into the sea, his friend asked, "Why are you doing that? With all the hundreds of miles of shoreline around the sea, there must be thousands of starfish that are dying right now. What good can throwing one little starfish really matter to the whole population of starfish?" The little boy stood there holding the starfish in his hand and said, "I'm not sure what it will do for all the rest of the starfish in the world, but it will mean the world to this one." He threw it back into the sea, and the starfish regained its life and went on to do its thing.

Can you make a difference to one person today? Can you

touch a single life? Can you stop a hurt? Can you turn one frown upside down? Can you see one fellow student in the cafeteria, who needs a friend, and go sit by her for ten to fifteen minutes? Can you lift your father's spirits just a little bit by saying, "I love you," and leaving him a note about all the things he does for you that you take for granted? Could your younger brother be that starfish? By merely letting him be with you for a few moments, play with you or your friend, be a part of your group, watch TV or a video with you—can you imagine what that might do to him and for him for the rest of his life?

I've always regretted not spending more time with my brother Dale as I grew up. I figured that all younger brothers were starfish that deserved to stay on the shore, begging in the hot sun, roasting under the pressures of life. Sure, they beg for just a drop of water, but I was riding my bike with my friends. Who wants a little kid tagging along? Besides, he was a threat. Dale did better in most sports, and though he was three years younger, he could beat me up, so no way was I going to take him with me. If I could have saved him a few times, we might have been better friends as we grew up. As it is, it took several years for us to get really close. Now in our thirties we are close, but only because we finally recognized each other as starfish who needed friends with helping hands.

Today I challenge you not to think about what you *can't* do. Focus on what you *can* do. You can make someone happy by noticing her clothes or mentioning one of his past accomplishments or achievements.

Not only are you a starfish, the little boy is God's Son. Second Peter 3:9 reminds you: ". . . He is patient with you, not wanting anyone to perish. . . ." Jesus covers every inch of the shorelines of lost souls, so He might save every one. God loves you. If people try and make you feel insignificant today, just remember that to God you are a priceless starfish.

68
Pressure From All the Wrong Places

Dear Mom and Dad: I really appreciate that you care so much about me. All your love and support really keep me going, but sometimes you push me so much that I can't take the pressure, and nothing goes well. Sincerely, Your Pressured Child.

I have so many worries that I have to deal with each day, that your pressuring me to be perfect is killing me. I'm seriously thinking about smoking, drinking, or getting high just to see what it's like.

Young people have enough pressure on them today without getting it from home. However, pressure from your parents is the one area you can do something about. You can't stop the world from pushing you to buy this or drink that, to get into pornography or the wars. You can't stop your peers from making alcohol and sex look fun and exciting, because—guess what?—it is! But you *can* look at the end result of those destructive elements and at your parents' pressure and do something about them.

1. *Talk.* You're becoming an adult. If you don't practice talking out your problems and concerns with your parents, how will you have any experience when it comes to your boss or spouse? One letter I received had been written by a teen who felt mad at his parents because they didn't put a sign up on the front yard that said, NO DOGS DUMPING; he blamed them for stepping in the stuff. Make sure your complaints are for real and go talk about them.
2. *Find a solution or compromise on some of your parents' pressures.* With God's help and your desire to grow, you can do it!

With love, give your parents these verses:

Colossians 3:21: Fathers, do not embitter your children, or they will become discouraged.

Ephesians 6:4: Fathers, do not exasperate your children; instead, bring them up in the training and instruction of the Lord.

69
Is It Really Cheating?

Dear Bill: I've heard it said that when you cheat on a test, you really cheat yourself. Do you really think that if a student looks over on another person's paper for just an answer or two out of an entire test, he is really hurting himself?

When I was in college, I took a management course—one I had to have to earn a business degree. This was a large lecture class with several hundred students. Each week we had to take a quiz. Throughout the semester the professor gave twelve to fifteen quizzes. You had to take at least 80 percent of them. Out of every ten quizzes, you could miss a couple.

One time, I was leaving town for the weekend with some friends. As I walked off campus, a classmate from this class came up and asked me if I would be at class that day. I told him no, I was leaving for the weekend.

"I'll be glad to take the quiz for you," he offered.

"No, that's okay."

"Really. No problem. Just give me your student I.D. number, and I'll take the quiz for you. I'll put your name and number on it and hand it in at the end of the class."

My first mistake was not thinking about his offer and thinking through my answer. My second mistake, probably a greater one, was not having integrity and honesty so built into my system that I wouldn't even have to think about such a ridiculous question. Since I was the king of my life during those days and listened to no one but myself and made many bad decisions because God was not guiding me (nor did I want Him to), I looked my classmate in the eye and said, "Sure . . . . Go ahead and do it. Here is my I.D. number."

I didn't even have to take that test. But I didn't really consider it cheating, because I didn't do anything. Oh, sure, I gave him consent, but he was going to do everything. Besides, he told me he had it all thought out and would take care of it. There wasn't even a professor in the room— just hundreds of students and a box in the back, where the tests went at the end of the hour. I figured it was a cinch and guaranteed to work.

A week later, after class was over, the professor announced he wanted to see Bill Sanders and the other fellow. We both walked into his office. He put both test papers on the table and said, "Both of you cheated." We acted innocent and said, "What do you mean?" He said, "Look. Both papers are identical." He also showed me where the other guy had written his name and I.D. on his paper—and on my paper he wrote his name, crossed it off, and put my name above it. It was very obvious what had happened.

The professor said, "Guess what both of you get to do?"

We asked, "What?"

"You get to take this class over again next year. This year you receive Fs. That will bring your grade-point averages down; it will be on your record that you got this F because of cheating; and this will go into your major and be on your college record forever."

I learned a very valuable lesson that day. First I learned that some friends are not really friends at all, because they don't even stand on sound principles. I also learned about the word cheating. I tried to justify that I wasn't really cheating and he was doing it for me, and there was no way we could get caught because he had it all figured out. It is like the story I hear from young people who get caught with drugs, driving too fast, or drinking while they are driving. Their friends seem to have it all figured out: "There is no way we can get caught. I've thought about it ahead of time." Baloney. Cheating is cheating. Cheating hurts you by tearing at your insides. It makes you realize that you are not really a great person. You would stoop to cheating or anything else to help yourself—no right or wrong, no morals, no "God's rules," just do your own thing. If it feels good, don't worry if you hurt anyone, and don't get caught.

You do hurt yourself if you cheat. I had to take the class

over again, and the second time I got a B. Put a B and an F together, and it averages out to be a D. I realized that it just wasn't worth it.

Honesty and integrity are things you can't buy—and people cannot take them from you. If someone asks you if you want to cheat or be a part of something you know is wrong, without a moment's hesitation, say, "Absolutely not. I am not going to compromise my values or myself for this, so I say *no.*"

I had a very costly lesson, and I hope you don't have to go through it. The next time you take a test and your eyes start to wander, remember that you will definitely hurt yourself. You might not get caught the way I did, but you will live with a broken part of yourself on the inside for a long time. It's just not worth it.

When you feel tempted to copy or cheat, remember that you are actually imitating the person you are copying:

3 John 11: Dear friend, do not imitate what is evil but what is good. Anyone who does what is good is from God. Anyone who does what is evil has not seen God.

Ephesians 5:1: Be imitators of God. . . .

If you want to copy someone, I think God's Word clearly shows who that should be!

70
"Doubt It"

"I feel so bad inside. I know I turned my life over to Jesus four years ago, but lately I have so many doubts. Am I really saved?" Have you ever doubted your relationship with God or your salvation? If so, you are normal. I have, and many others whom I know and read about also say they've doubted.

Did you know that Jesus said, "There is no one greater than this," about a man who had doubts about Him? Though he knew Jesus personally and had the great honor baptizing Him, John the Baptist, Jesus' second cousin wondered if He really was what He claimed to be. At that baptism, John had seen the Holy Spirit descend and heard God say, "I am pleased with My Son." Though John had told several of his followers to follow Jesus instead of himself and knew Jesus to be God's Son, now that he was in prison, he had a lot of questions. After only a few months, John began to ask his friends to go and ask Jesus if He was the expected Savior and Messiah of the Old Testament. *Should I look for another?* he wondered. Can you imagine? Such a great prophet as John the Baptist, in doubt!

When I doubted my salvation, another Christian directed

me to Romans 10:9, 10. Look it up and know for sure that you are God's child. If you can say, "Jesus is my Lord," and you believe He was raised from the dead, you are saved. The key word is *Lord.* Money, popularity, vanity, or the world cannot be your lord—only Jesus!

How did John have his doubts removed? Jesus told John's friends to return to the prison and report all His miracles back to John. They did, and John was reassured. Why? Because they were the same miracles written about in the Old Testament about the Coming King. (Read about both accounts in Luke 7:18–23 and Isaiah 35:3–6.)

The next time you say, "I doubt it and feel bad about it," look it up in the book and talk to the Author.

71

A Christmas Gift— Cancer?

One Christmas, I couldn't understand why my father was sick. The doctors said he would not make it through the week, the cancer was too thick in his stomach, and he could not be operated on. A year later, I knew all this came about so our family could be healed and brought together. In that sickbed, I saw my father accept Jesus Christ as his Lord and

Savior. Two months later, he walked the aisle of our church and joined the church with my mother—both in their seventies. About a month after that, on one of the neatest days of my life, I saw them get baptized. My younger brother and my older brother made up and became friends and said, "I love you," for the first time in a long time. For the first time in over twelve years, I cried. Three older sisters whom I love dearly shared things they had been feeling about one another, hurts and pains and forgivenesses, that would never have been brought out otherwise. My family, restored and strengthened, stopped taking God's blessings for granted at least for a little while. We couldn't see the good at the time, but as I look back I can see it all.

If someone in your family is physically sick or hurting or emotionally scarred, pray. Let the Lord be your strength and remember there is good in there somewhere. Dig in and find it. It may be in an unfamiliar package, but once you unwrap it, you'll find His "gift."

Isaiah 55:8: "For my thoughts are not your thoughts, neither are your ways my ways," declares the Lord.

72
"Stand Up" at the Bottom

Recently a woman told me about all the bad things that have happened to her family. After a school assembly, a young boy came up to me and shared that he had lost his family in a car accident, and he was all alone in this world. On the news I've heard several accounts of disasters, in which only one family member was left alive. What do we do when troubles and tragedies hit? Where do we find strength and comfort?

If you feel down in the dumps, with garbage piling in all around, if you see very little sunshine, hope, and no hands reaching down, please concentrate on the following verses from the One who put the stars in their place, was surrounded with troubles, and hung in our place on the jagged, sharp, wooden cross, almost two thousand years ago.

Nahum 1:7: The Lord is good, a refuge in times of trouble. He cares for those who trust in him.

John 14:1: "Do not let your hearts be troubled. Trust in God; trust also in me."

2 Corinthians 4:8, 9: We are hard pressed on every side, but not crushed; perplexed, but not in despair; persecuted, but not abandoned; struck down, but not destroyed.

Psalms 138:7: Though I walk in the midst of trouble, you preserve my life; you stretch out your hand against the anger of my foes, with your right hand you save me.

Isaiah 43:2: When you pass through the waters, I will be with you; and when you pass through the rivers, they will not sweep over you. When you walk through the fire, you will not be burned; the flames will not set you ablaze.

Psalms 121:1, 2: I lift up my eyes to the hills—where does my help come from? My help comes from the Lord, the Maker of heaven and earth.

Romans 8:28: And we know that in all things God works for the good of those who love him, who have been called according to his purpose.

Hebrews 4:15, 16: For we do not have a high priest who is unable to sympathize with our weaknesses, but we have one who has been tempted in every way, just as we are—yet was without sin. Let us then approach the throne of grace with confidence, so that we may receive mercy and find grace to help us in our time of need.

1 Peter 5:7: Cast all your anxiety on him because he cares for you.

God knows what it feels like to be tempted, troubled, and treated like dirt. He also offers us strength and hope, a hand to hang on to, and a word of encouragement when we need it. Next time you feel down and out, with no light switch nearby to turn on, look at those verses again.

When you're at the bottom, God doesn't provide a hot air balloon to raise you up, but He does hand you a ladder. Just stand up and start climbing.

Psalms 119:105: Your word is a lamp to my feet and a light for my path.

73
I Can Be Just Like You

Josh McDowell was recently in Kalamazoo, giving a talk on his national campaign called "Sex—Why Wait?" Before his talk, I saw Josh in the lobby. We encouraged each other for a few brief moments, and I went and prayed for him as he prepared to talk.

That night Josh told me a story about a girl who was ridiculed by many kids in her school, because she was still a virgin. She almost became ashamed of the fact, until she went to hear Josh speak. He told her that when God tells us not to do something, such as not having sex before marriage, He isn't being a killjoy and keeping us from fun. Two principles always form the basis of God's saying, "Do not do this," or, "Do not do that." First, God wants to protect us. In the case of sex, He wants to protect us from the memories that will linger forever and ever, low self-esteem, various diseases, and so on. Second, He wants to give us His provision. He wants to provide us with a healthy way of life and with His beauty, which we can live out as we go through life, with His protection, His love, and His care. God's provision is in every verse where He tells us not to do something.

This girl found a new strength. Maybe for the first time in her life she felt proud of being a virgin. She was proud of the fact that the greatest gift that she could give her husband when she got married some day was her virginity. They could learn sex together.

Josh challenges everyone to be a pro at relationships, but an amateur at sex. He says, "Maybe you won't even have sex on your wedding night, but it will bind you together like nothing else can. You will be close and have a strength or friendship that will not blow away with the nearest, earliest, or quickest rain or wind." The girl went back to school and told her friends that their making fun of her virginity would never again intimidate her. She told them never to attack her virginity or what she stands for. What she said has given me great hope and strength to stand for what I believe. She looked at the other girls who tried to get her to be just like them, to get her to be a "real woman" and have sex, to get her to quit being old-fashioned and stay home all the time or turn guys off and say she wasn't going to have sex until she was married and said, "I can be like you anytime I want. I can lose my virginity any weekend I wish, but none of you can ever again be like me!"

That is powerful! God wants us to have His power, His strength, His courage and convictions Please don't give in just because everyone else is doing it. In fact, the next time a guy says everyone else is doing it just tell him, "Then it shouldn't be hard for you to find someone else to do it with!" If a guy says, "Do you want to get in the backseat?" tell him, "No, I'm happy to be right up here in the front seat with you." I must admit Josh gives me some good one-liners as well. I thank him for awakening an entire nation and being away from his family many days because he cares about you. Grab his book *Why Wait?* It covers what you need to know about the teen sexuality crisis. It will change your life—it has mine!

74
Why Am I Jealous?

The Compact Encyclopedia of Psychological Problems, by Clyde M. Narramore, defines jealousy as: "An attitude of envy or resentment toward a more successful rival. Feelings of jealousy are usually the result of frustration in attempts to achieve a desired object."

The author also describes several causes of jealousy that can help you analyze yourself or someone you know. Jealousy can result from:

1. The way your parents handle early relationships in your childhood. If your parents compared you, put you down, or made it obvious that you did not do as well as your brother or sister, this could have caused jealousy that can linger on for many years.

2. The coming of a brother or sister. When you were younger and a new baby brother or sister came along, all of a sudden you were not number one. All the time in the world wasn't spent with you by your parents, and therefore you may have become very jealous.

3. Excessive competition. If your parents challenge you to do

too much or to live up to their images, or be this or that on the court or the field, or get grades that would equal theirs, to become a doctor or whatever, this could also bring on some inside insecurities that result in jealousy.

4. *Parental favoritism.* If your parents play favorites, you may become jealous.

5. *Feelings of insecurity and inadequacy.* Quite often jealousy has to do with each one of us comparing ourselves with others. We wouldn't do that if we felt secure and adequate —if we felt we were okay as we were.

6. *A lack of spiritual development.* When a person's thoughts are not controlled by Christ, he tends to compare his situation to others'. Then being envious or jealous is only a natural outcome.

Mark 7:21–23: "For from within, out of men's hearts, come evil thoughts, sexual immorality, theft, murder, adultery, greed, malice, deceit, lewdness, envy, slander, arrogance and folly. All these evils come from inside and make a man 'unclean.'"

Why should anyone who believes in Christ as Savior and who has the creator of the universe living in his heart be jealous of anyone else? Maybe from time to time he should feel sorry for others—sorry enough, that is, to help them. Maybe he admires someone and where he has gotten in life because of hard work, stick-to-it-iveness, the ability to care for others, and the ability to carry on a dream when impossible odds faced him. These are great things to try to emulate and pull into his own life, but he shouldn't waste time being jealous. You, too, have better things for your time and your life. Remember, from within out of the heart of men proceed these evil thoughts, and jealousy is one of them.

75
Why I Like My Parents

Dear Bill: I guess I am one of the fortunate ones. Today I heard you talk about ways in which we can get to know our parents better and understand them, as well as learn from them, and I am one who didn't need your talk. I love my parents, and it seems they have done so many things just right—the way you said in your talk. Here are some of the things that I like best about my parents: (1) Whenever I hurt, they are always there. They never talk down to me, and they truly want to listen to my troubles and pains. (2) If they say it, they mean it. My parents never tell me one thing and do another. (3) They don't compare me to my brothers or sisters, because they know each of us are individuals and have strong and weak points. They help us focus on our strong points and never say we aren't as good as another brother or sister. (4) They are never too busy for me. We go on vacations together and almost every day spend some time talking together. Whenever they say they will do something with me, they write it down in an appointment book. It is as important to them as anything else. (5) They have made our home a happy place. My friends come over all the time. My parents are easy to laugh with, enjoy, talk to, and listen to. All my friends think I am the luckiest person in the world, and you know what? So do I!

Have you ever written down the things that you like about your parents? Letters like this are very refreshing. Each of us *could* write such a list, but we never take the time. It seems easier to think about the negatives. Get a sheet of paper and write down three or four things that you appreciate about your mom and dad. Forget about the things they goof up. Maybe by focusing on their good points and telling them that you appreciate them, you will start to fall in love with your parents like never before. You may realize they care for you like no other people on the face of this earth, and you might help them focus on *your* positive points, instead of the negative ones. It is a two-way street. Get the ball rolling.

Philippians 4:8: "Finally, brothers [sisters], whatever is true, whatever is noble, whatever is right, whatever is pure, whatever is lovely, whatever is admirable—if anything is excellent or praiseworthy—think about such things."

If you have any questions or problems you wish to share, please drop me a note at:

Bill Sanders
P.O. Box 711
Portage, MI 49081